Emotional Intelligence

Unlocking Your Potential for Personal and Professional Success

Emotional Intelligence

Unlocking Your Potential for Personal and Professional Success

Dr. N. Gosain

The Readers Paradise
New Delhi - 110002

Emotional Intelligence
Dr. N. Gosain

ISBN - 978-93-5977-055-0

Published by The Readers Paradise
www.thereadersparadise.com

Printed and Bound in India

Cover Design by Kamini Bijoria

Typeset by The Readers Paradise

First Edition: 2024

Preface

In an ever-evolving world where the ability to connect, communicate, and collaborate is paramount, emotional intelligence (EI) emerges as a cornerstone of success. "Emotional Intelligence: Unlocking Your Potential for Personal and Professional Success" is designed to guide you on a transformative journey towards understanding and mastering this essential skill set.

This book is more than a mere exploration of emotional intelligence; it is a practical toolkit that equips you with the insights and strategies needed to harness your emotions effectively. Through the chapters, you will explore into the core components of EI—self-awareness, self-regulation, motivation, empathy, and social skills—discovering how each plays a crucial role in both your personal and professional life.

You will learn how emotional intelligence can enhance your relationships, improve workplace dynamics, and contribute positively to your mental health. The cultural and social perspectives presented will enrich your understanding of how emotional intelligence operates within diverse contexts, while our worksheets and exercises provide hands-on practice to reinforce your learning.

As you navigate through the pages, my hope is that you uncover your unique emotional strengths and learn to turn challenges into opportunities for growth. Whether you are a seasoned professional looking to refine your skills or someone seeking to enhance your personal relationships, this book offers a pathway to deeper self-understanding and meaningful connections.

Join me in unlocking the potential that lies within you. Let's embark on this journey towards emotional intelligence together, paving the way for greater fulfillment and success in all aspects of life.

— Author

Contents

Preface

1

Self-Awareness

What is Self-Awareness?

Self-awareness is the cornerstone of emotional intelligence and a fundamental aspect of personal growth and development. It involves the ability to recognize and understand one's own emotions, thoughts, values, strengths, weaknesses, and motivations. This self-insight enables individuals to navigate life's challenges more effectively, make informed decisions, and cultivate fulfilling relationships.

At its essence, self-awareness involves turning our attention inward and observing our internal experiences without judgment or bias. It requires a willingness to explore our thoughts, feelings, and behaviors with honesty and curiosity, seeking to understand the underlying factors driving our actions and reactions.

Self-aware individuals possess a deep understanding

of their emotions, including their triggers, intensity, and impact on behavior. They can accurately identify their emotional states in real-time, allowing them to respond to situations with clarity and composure rather than reacting impulsively or defensively.

Furthermore, self-awareness extends beyond mere emotional recognition to encompass a broader understanding of oneself, including one's values, beliefs, and identity. This self-understanding provides a sense of purpose and direction, guiding individuals in aligning their actions with their core values and aspirations.

Self-awareness also involves an awareness of one's strengths and weaknesses. Recognizing our strengths allows us to leverage them effectively, building on our areas of competence and expertise. Conversely, acknowledging our weaknesses enables us to identify areas for growth and development, fostering a mindset of continuous learning and improvement.

Cultivating self-awareness is an ongoing process that requires introspection, reflection, and self-exploration. Practices such as mindfulness meditation, journaling, and self-assessment can help individuals develop greater self-awareness by fostering present-moment awareness and nonjudgmental self-observation.

In addition to individual introspection, feedback from others plays a crucial role in enhancing self-awareness. Seeking input from trusted friends, mentors, or colleagues can provide valuable insights into our blind spots and areas for development, offering perspectives that may not be apparent from self-reflection alone.

Ultimately, self-awareness empowers individuals to take ownership of their thoughts, feelings, and actions, leading to greater self-confidence, resilience, and authenticity. By cultivating self-awareness, we can cultivate deeper self-understanding, forge more meaningful connections with others, and lead more fulfilling and purpose-driven lives.

Importance of Self-Awareness

Self-awareness is not just a desirable trait; it's a foundational element for personal growth, meaningful relationships, and overall well-being. Its importance spans across various aspects of life, influencing how individuals perceive themselves, interact with others, and navigate the complexities of the world around them.

At its core, self-awareness involves the ability to recognize and understand one's own thoughts, emotions, strengths, weaknesses, values, and motivations. This introspective insight serves as a compass, guiding individuals in making informed decisions, setting meaningful goals, and aligning their actions with their core values and aspirations.

One of the key benefits of self-awareness is its role in fostering emotional intelligence. By being attuned to their own emotions, individuals can better regulate their emotional responses, manage stress effectively, and maintain a sense of balance and resilience in the face of adversity. This emotional self-awareness also enables individuals to empathize with others, understand their perspectives, and navigate social interactions with empathy and compassion.

Self-awareness is also essential for personal growth and development. When individuals have a deep understanding of their strengths and weaknesses, they can capitalize on their strengths while actively working to improve upon their areas of weakness. This self-insight fuels a growth mindset, encouraging individuals to embrace challenges, seek feedback, and continuously strive for self-improvement.

In addition to personal growth, self-awareness plays a crucial role in fostering authentic and fulfilling relationships. When individuals have a clear understanding of themselves, they are better equipped to communicate their needs, boundaries, and expectations to others. This transparency and authenticity lay the foundation for healthy and mutually supportive relationships built on trust, respect, and empathy.

Furthermore, self-awareness is instrumental in decision-making and problem-solving. When individuals understand their own values, priorities, and goals, they can make decisions that are aligned with their long-term interests and aspirations. This self-clarity helps individuals navigate complex choices and overcome decision paralysis by staying true to themselves and their vision.

Moreover, self-awareness fosters resilience and adaptability in the face of change. By being attuned to their own thoughts and emotions, individuals can navigate transitions, setbacks, and challenges with greater ease and grace. Rather than being swept away by external circumstances, they can maintain a sense of inner stability and perspective, drawing upon their self-awareness to navigate turbulent waters with resilience and courage.

Self-awareness also enhances leadership effectiveness. Leaders who possess a deep understanding of themselves are better equipped to inspire and motivate others, build trust and rapport, and navigate complex interpersonal dynamics. By leading with authenticity and integrity, they create an environment that fosters collaboration, innovation, and collective success.

Self-Awareness vs. Self-Consciousness

Self-awareness and self-consciousness are two related but distinct concepts in psychology, each with its own implications for behavior, cognition, and emotional well-being. Understanding the differences between these concepts can shed light on how individuals perceive themselves and interact with the world around them.

Self-Awareness:

Self-awareness refers to the ability to recognize, understand, and reflect on one's own thoughts, emotions, strengths, weaknesses, values, and motivations. It involves introspective insight and a deep understanding of oneself, including one's identity, beliefs, and desires.

1. **Internal Focus**: Self-awareness involves turning one's attention inward and engaging in self-reflection to gain insight into one's inner experiences. It requires a willingness to explore one's thoughts, feelings, and behaviors with honesty and curiosity.
2. **Insight and Understanding**: Self-aware individuals possess a clear understanding of their own emotions, motivations, and tendencies. They can accurately identify their emotional states, recognize their strengths and weaknesses, and understand how their thoughts and behaviors influence their actions and interactions with others.
3. **Emotional Intelligence**: Self-awareness is a cornerstone of emotional intelligence, enabling individuals to regulate their emotions effectively, manage stress, and navigate social interactions with empathy and compassion.

Self-Consciousness:

Self-consciousness, on the other hand, refers to a heightened awareness of oneself in relation to others or to social norms and expectations. It involves a focus on how one is perceived by others and a tendency to self-monitor or evaluate one's behavior in social situations.

1. **External Focus**: Self-consciousness involves directing one's attention outward, toward how one is perceived by others or how one's behavior aligns with societal norms. It often leads to a heightened sensitivity to social cues and a concern for how one is being judged by others.
2. **Social Comparison**: Self-conscious individuals may engage in social comparison, evaluating themselves in relation to others and seeking validation or approval from external sources. This can lead to feelings of insecurity or self-doubt if one perceives oneself as falling short of societal standards or expectations.
3. **Performance Anxiety**: Self-consciousness can also manifest as performance anxiety or self-doubt in social or evaluative situations. Individuals may become overly concerned with making a good impression or avoiding embarrassment, leading to self-conscious behaviors such as blushing, fidgeting, or avoiding eye contact.

Both self-awareness and self-consciousness involve an awareness of oneself, they differ in focus and orientation. Self-awareness is inwardly directed, involving introspective insight and self-understanding, while self-consciousness is outwardly directed, involving a heightened awareness of how one is perceived by others or how one's behavior conforms to social norms. While self-awareness is generally seen as a positive trait associated with emotional intelligence and personal growth, excessive self-consciousness can lead to anxiety, self-doubt, and social inhibition.

Developing Self-Awareness

Developing self-awareness is a transformative journey that involves deep introspection, reflection, and a commitment to understanding oneself on a profound level. While it may seem daunting at first, cultivating self-awareness is an invaluable investment in personal growth, emotional intelligence, and overall well-being. Here are some strategies and practices to help you embark on this journey:

1. **Practice Mindfulness**: Mindfulness involves paying attention to the present moment with openness and nonjudgmental awareness. Engaging in mindfulness meditation or mindfulness exercises can help you become more attuned to your thoughts, emotions, and bodily sensations, fostering greater self-awareness.
2. **Journaling**: Keeping a journal allows you to reflect on your thoughts, feelings, and experiences in a private and nonjudgmental space. Writing regularly about your inner experiences can help you gain insights into patterns, triggers, and underlying emotions, deepening your self-awareness over time.
3. **Seek Feedback**: Actively seek feedback from trusted friends, family members, or mentors who can provide honest and constructive insights into your strengths, weaknesses, and blind spots. Be open to receiving feedback with curiosity and a willingness to learn and grow.
4. **Self-Reflection Exercises**: Set aside time for self-reflection exercises, such as asking yourself reflective questions or engaging in guided introspection. Consider questions like "What are my core values?" or "What motivates me?" These exercises can help you gain clarity and deepen your understanding of yourself.
5. **Practice Emotional Awareness**: Pay attention to your emotions as they arise throughout the day. Notice the physical sensations, thoughts, and

triggers associated with each emotion. Developing emotional awareness can help you recognize patterns, regulate your emotions more effectively, and make informed decisions.

6. **Explore Your Strengths and Weaknesses**: Take time to identify your strengths, talents, and areas of expertise, as well as your weaknesses and areas for growth. Reflect on how these qualities influence your actions, interactions, and choices, and consider how you can leverage your strengths while actively working on your weaknesses.

7. **Engage in Self-Assessment Tools**: Consider using self-assessment tools or personality assessments to gain insights into your personality traits, preferences, and tendencies. While these tools are not definitive, they can provide valuable insights and starting points for self-reflection.

8. **Cultivate Empathy**: Develop empathy by putting yourself in others' shoes and considering their perspectives, feelings, and experiences. Practicing empathy can deepen your understanding of others and enhance your interpersonal relationships, while also fostering greater self-awareness as you explore how you relate to others.

9. **Embrace Vulnerability**: Be willing to embrace vulnerability and authenticity in your interactions with yourself and others. Acknowledge your imperfections, fears, and insecurities with compassion and self-acceptance, recognizing that vulnerability is an essential part of the human experience.

10. **Set Intentions for Growth**: Cultivate a growth mindset by setting intentions for personal growth and self-improvement. Approach challenges, setbacks, and failures as opportunities for

learning and growth, and celebrate your progress along the way.

Remember that developing self-awareness is an ongoing process that requires patience, commitment, and self-compassion. By cultivating self-awareness, you can gain deeper insights into yourself, enhance your relationships, and live a more authentic and fulfilling life.

Reflective Practices

Reflective practices are intentional activities or processes that encourage individuals to engage in self-reflection, critical thinking, and learning from their experiences. These practices are essential for personal and professional development, fostering self-awareness, insight, and continuous improvement. Here are some reflective practices and their benefits:

1. **Journaling**: Keeping a reflective journal allows individuals to record their thoughts, feelings, and experiences in a structured format. Writing regularly helps clarify thoughts, identify patterns, and gain insights into one's beliefs, values, and behaviors. Journaling can also serve as a tool for setting goals, tracking progress, and processing emotions.

2. **Mindfulness Meditation**: Mindfulness meditation involves paying attention to the present moment with openness and nonjudgmental awareness. Practicing mindfulness cultivates self-awareness, emotional regulation, and mental clarity. By observing thoughts, emotions, and sensations as they arise, individuals develop a deeper understanding of their inner experiences and learn to respond more skillfully to life's challenges.

3. **Critical Incident Analysis**: Critical incident analysis involves reflecting on specific events or

experiences to extract lessons and insights for future practice. By examining both successful and challenging situations, individuals can identify what worked well, what could be improved, and what lessons can be applied in similar contexts. Critical incident analysis promotes continuous learning and professional growth.

4. **Peer Feedback and Discussion**: Engaging in discussions with peers or colleagues provides opportunities for receiving feedback, sharing perspectives, and gaining new insights. Peer feedback fosters collaboration, mutual support, and collective learning. By listening to different viewpoints and experiences, individuals broaden their perspectives and deepen their understanding of themselves and others.
5. **Coaching and Mentoring**: Working with a coach or mentor provides personalized support and guidance for self-reflection and professional development. Coaches and mentors ask probing questions, challenge assumptions, and provide feedback to help individuals gain clarity, set goals, and navigate challenges. Through coaching and mentoring relationships, individuals gain new perspectives, insights, and strategies for growth.
6. **Self-Assessment Tools**: Utilizing self-assessment tools or surveys can provide valuable insights into one's personality, strengths, preferences, and areas for development. These tools offer a structured framework for self-reflection and self-awareness, helping individuals identify their unique qualities and navigate their career paths more effectively.
7. **Reflective Writing Assignments**: In educational settings, reflective writing assignments prompt students to critically analyze their learning

experiences, coursework, and professional practice. Reflective writing encourages students to articulate their thoughts, reflect on their learning process, and integrate new knowledge into their existing understanding. These assignments promote metacognition, self-regulation, and deep learning.

8. **Regular Check-Ins**: Setting aside time for regular self-check-ins allows individuals to assess their progress, evaluate their goals, and adjust their strategies as needed. By pausing to reflect on their achievements, challenges, and aspirations, individuals maintain a sense of direction and purpose in their personal and professional lives.

Reflective practices are essential for promoting self-awareness, critical thinking, and continuous learning. By engaging in intentional reflection, individuals gain deeper insights into themselves, their experiences, and their environments, empowering them to make informed decisions, navigate challenges, and pursue their goals with clarity and purpose.

Mindfulness and Meditation

Mindfulness and meditation are closely related practices that involve cultivating present-moment awareness, focused attention, and nonjudgmental acceptance. While they share similarities, they also have distinct characteristics and benefits. Let's explore each practice:

Mindfulness:

Mindfulness is the practice of paying attention to the present moment with openness, curiosity, and acceptance. It involves being fully engaged in whatever is happening in the here and now, without getting caught up in thoughts about the past or worries about the future. Mindfulness can be practiced formally through meditation exercises, as well as informally in daily activities such as eating, walking, or listening.

Key Characteristics of Mindfulness:

1. **Present-Moment Awareness**: Mindfulness involves intentionally directing attention to the sensations, thoughts, and emotions occurring in the present moment, without clinging to or rejecting them.

2. **Nonjudgmental Acceptance**: Mindfulness encourages an attitude of openness and acceptance toward one's experiences, including both pleasant and unpleasant sensations, thoughts, and emotions.

3. **Focused Attention**: Mindfulness practices often involve focusing attention on a specific anchor, such as the breath, bodily sensations, or sounds, to cultivate sustained attention and awareness.

Benefits of Mindfulness:

1. **Stress Reduction**: Mindfulness practices have been shown to reduce stress levels by promoting relaxation, reducing rumination, and increasing resilience to stressors.

2. **Emotional Regulation**: Mindfulness enhances emotional awareness and regulation, allowing individuals to respond more skillfully to challenging emotions and situations.

3. **Improved Concentration**: Regular mindfulness practice strengthens attentional control and cognitive functioning, leading to improved concentration, focus, and productivity.

4. **Enhanced Well-Being**: Mindfulness is associated with greater overall well-being, including increased satisfaction with life, improved relationships, and greater psychological resilience.

Meditation:

Meditation refers to a diverse set of practices that cultivate focused attention, relaxation, and mental clarity. While mindfulness meditation is one form of meditation, there are many other types, including concentration meditation, loving-kindness meditation, and transcendental meditation.

Key Characteristics of Meditation:

1. **Focused Attention**: Meditation practices typically involve directing attention to a specific object of focus, such as the breath, a mantra, or a visual image, to cultivate concentration and awareness.
2. **Relaxation and Tranquility**: Meditation techniques promote relaxation and tranquility by calming the mind, reducing mental chatter, and inducing a state of deep relaxation.
3. **Deepening Awareness**: Meditation practices deepen self-awareness and insight by quieting the mind, allowing individuals to observe their thoughts, emotions, and sensations more clearly.

Benefits of Meditation:

1. **Stress Reduction**: Like mindfulness, meditation is effective for reducing stress and promoting relaxation, leading to a greater sense of calm and well-being.
2. **Improved Mental Health**: Regular meditation practice is associated with reduced symptoms of anxiety, depression, and other mental health conditions, as well as increased emotional resilience and self-regulation.
3. **Enhanced Cognitive Functioning**: Meditation enhances cognitive functioning, including attention, memory, and executive function, leading to improved decision-making and problem-solving abilities.

4. **Spiritual Growth**: For many people, meditation is a spiritual practice that fosters a sense of connection, meaning, and purpose in life, leading to greater spiritual growth and fulfillment.

Mindfulness and meditation are powerful practices for cultivating present-moment awareness, relaxation, and well-being. While mindfulness emphasizes nonjudgmental awareness of the present moment, meditation involves various techniques for focused attention and mental clarity. Both practices offer numerous benefits for physical, emotional, and spiritual health, making them valuable tools for personal growth and transformation.

Journaling and Self-Reflection Exercises

Journaling and self-reflection exercises are powerful tools for fostering self-awareness, personal growth, and emotional well-being. Both practices provide structured ways to explore thoughts, feelings, and experiences, leading to greater insight and understanding of oneself. Let's delve into each practice and explore their benefits:

Journaling:

Journaling involves the regular practice of writing down thoughts, feelings, and experiences in a journal or diary. It provides a safe and private space for self-expression and exploration. There are many different approaches to journaling, including free writing, gratitude journaling, and reflective journaling.

Key Characteristics of Journaling:

1. **Self-Expression**: Journaling allows individuals to express themselves freely and openly without fear of judgment. It provides an outlet for processing emotions, thoughts, and experiences.
2. **Reflection and Insight**: Through journaling, individuals can reflect on past events, gain

insights into patterns and behaviors, and explore deeper meanings behind their experiences.

3. **Goal Setting and Tracking**: Journaling can be used as a tool for setting goals, tracking progress, and celebrating achievements. Writing down goals and action plans increases accountability and motivation.

Benefits of Journaling:

1. **Emotional Regulation**: Journaling helps individuals process and manage difficult emotions by providing a space to explore and express them in a healthy way. It can also promote a sense of catharsis and relief.
2. **Stress Reduction**: Regular journaling has been shown to reduce stress levels by promoting relaxation, clarity, and perspective. It allows individuals to release pent-up emotions and gain a sense of control over their thoughts and feelings.
3. **Increased Self-Awareness**: Journaling promotes self-awareness by encouraging individuals to reflect on their thoughts, feelings, and behaviors. It helps uncover underlying beliefs, values, and motivations, leading to greater self-understanding.
4. **Enhanced Creativity and Problem-Solving**: Engaging in creative writing exercises or brainstorming sessions in a journal can stimulate creativity and innovation. Journaling can also help individuals brainstorm solutions to challenges or explore new ideas.

Self-Reflection Exercises:

Self-reflection exercises involve structured activities or prompts designed to encourage introspection, self-awareness, and personal growth. These exercises can take various forms, including guided visualization, self-assessment questionnaires, and reflective prompts.

Key Characteristics of Self-Reflection Exercises:

1. **Introspection**: Self-reflection exercises encourage individuals to explore their thoughts, feelings, and experiences in depth. They provide a framework for deepening self-awareness and gaining insights into one's inner world.
2. **Critical Thinking**: Self-reflection exercises promote critical thinking by encouraging individuals to analyze their thoughts, beliefs, and behaviors from different perspectives. They challenge assumptions and encourage open-mindedness.
3. **Goal Alignment**: Self-reflection exercises help individuals clarify their goals, values, and priorities, leading to greater alignment between actions and intentions. They facilitate decision-making and goal setting by fostering self-awareness and self-knowledge.

Benefits of Self-Reflection Exercises:

1. **Increased Self-Awareness**: Self-reflection exercises promote self-awareness by encouraging individuals to explore their thoughts, feelings, and behaviors. They help uncover underlying beliefs, values, and motivations, leading to greater self-understanding.
2. **Personal Growth and Development**: Engaging in self-reflection exercises fosters personal growth and development by encouraging individuals to learn from their experiences, identify areas for improvement, and set goals for self-improvement.
3. **Enhanced Problem-Solving Skills**: Self-reflection exercises help individuals develop problem-solving skills by encouraging them to analyze situations, identify challenges, and brainstorm potential

solutions. They promote critical thinking and creative problem-solving.

4. **Improved Decision-Making**: By fostering self-awareness and self-understanding, self-reflection exercises help individuals make more informed and intentional decisions. They encourage individuals to consider their values, priorities, and long-term goals when making choices.

Journaling and self-reflection exercises are valuable practices for fostering self-awareness, personal growth, and emotional well-being. Both practices provide structured ways to explore thoughts, feelings, and experiences, leading to greater insight and understanding of oneself. By engaging in regular journaling and self-reflection, individuals can cultivate a deeper connection with themselves, develop greater self-awareness, and make more intentional choices in their lives.

2

Self-Regulation

Understanding Self-Regulation

Self-regulation, often referred to as self-control or self-management, is a fundamental aspect of human behavior that plays a crucial role in various domains of life, including personal development, academic achievement, emotional well-being, and social relationships. It encompasses the ability to monitor, manage, and modulate one's thoughts, emotions, impulses, and behaviors in accordance with internal standards, goals, and societal norms. Understanding self-regulation is essential for navigating the complexities of daily life, achieving long-term goals, and fostering resilience in the face of challenges.

Key Concepts of Self-Regulation

Self-regulation involves a complex interplay of cognitive, emotional, and behavioral processes, each contributing to an individual's ability to control and regulate their responses to internal and external stimuli. Key concepts related to self-regulation include:

1. **Executive Functions**: Self-regulation relies heavily on executive functions, which encompass cognitive processes such as attentional control, inhibition, working memory, and cognitive flexibility. These functions enable individuals to plan, organize, and execute goal-directed behaviors, resist distractions, and adapt to changing circumstances.

2. **Emotional Regulation**: Emotion regulation is an integral component of self-regulation, involving the ability to monitor, evaluate, and modulate one's emotional responses. Effective emotion regulation allows individuals to manage stress, cope with negative emotions, and maintain emotional balance in various situations.

3. **Impulse Control**: Self-regulation involves the ability to resist immediate gratification and delay gratification in pursuit of long-term goals. Strong impulse control enables individuals to overcome temptations, make prudent decisions, and exercise self-discipline in the face of distractions or impulses.

4. **Self-Monitoring**: Self-regulation requires ongoing self-monitoring and self-awareness, allowing individuals to assess their own thoughts, emotions, and behaviors in real-time. Self-monitoring involves keeping track of one's progress, identifying areas for improvement, and adjusting strategies as needed to stay on course.

Development of Self-Regulation

The development of self-regulation begins in early childhood and continues throughout the lifespan, with significant changes occurring during key developmental stages. Infants and toddlers gradually learn to regulate their emotions and impulses with parental guidance and support, laying the foundation for more sophisticated self-regulation skills in later years.

As children grow older, they acquire increasingly complex self-regulation skills through a combination of biological maturation, socialization, and environmental influences. School-age children learn to regulate their attention, behavior, and emotions in academic settings, while adolescents face new challenges related to identity formation, peer relationships, and decision-making.

During adulthood, individuals continue to refine their self-regulation skills through education, work, and life experiences. They learn to set goals, manage time effectively, and cope with stress in a way that aligns with their values and priorities. However, self-regulation abilities may fluctuate depending on situational factors, cognitive load, and emotional state.

Importance of Self-Regulation

Self-regulation is essential for achieving personal and academic success, maintaining physical and mental health, and fostering positive relationships with others. Individuals who possess strong self-regulation skills are better equipped to:

1. **Achieve Goals**: Self-regulation enables individuals to set realistic goals, make plans, and take action to achieve desired outcomes. It helps them stay focused, motivated, and persistent in the face of obstacles or setbacks.
2. **Manage Stress**: Effective self-regulation allows individuals to cope with stressors and adversity in a healthy and adaptive manner. It helps reduce the negative impact of stress on physical and mental well-being, promoting resilience and psychological flexibility.

3. **Regulate Emotions**: Self-regulation plays a crucial role in managing emotions and interpersonal relationships. It allows individuals to express emotions appropriately, empathize with others, and resolve conflicts constructively.
4. **Make Sound Decisions**: Self-regulation helps individuals make informed and rational decisions by weighing the pros and cons, considering long-term consequences, and resisting impulsive or reckless behavior.

In summary, understanding self-regulation is essential for navigating the complexities of daily life, achieving long-term goals, and fostering resilience in the face of challenges. By cultivating self-awareness, developing executive functions, and practicing emotion regulation, individuals can enhance their self-regulation skills and lead more fulfilling and successful lives.

Key Aspects of Self-Regulation

Self-regulation is a complex psychological process that involves the ability to monitor, manage, and control one's thoughts, emotions, impulses, and behaviors. It encompasses a range of cognitive, emotional, and behavioral skills that enable individuals to regulate their internal states and responses to external stimuli. Understanding the key aspects of self-regulation is essential for cultivating this critical skill and promoting personal growth, achievement, and well-being.

1. **Executive Functions**: Self-regulation relies heavily on executive functions, which are higher-order cognitive processes that govern goal-directed behavior, decision-making, and self-control. These functions include attentional control, inhibition, working memory, cognitive flexibility, and planning. Executive functions enable individuals to set goals, make plans, and execute strategies to achieve desired outcomes.

2. **Emotional Regulation**: Emotion regulation is a central component of self-regulation, involving the ability to monitor, evaluate, and modulate one's emotional responses. Effective emotion regulation allows individuals to manage stress, cope with negative emotions, and maintain emotional balance in various situations. Emotion regulation strategies include cognitive reappraisal, expressive suppression, and mindfulness.

3. **Impulse Control**: Self-regulation requires the ability to resist immediate gratification and delay gratification in pursuit of long-term goals. Strong impulse control enables individuals to overcome temptations, resist distractions, and make prudent decisions that align with their values and priorities. Impulse control is associated with better academic and career success, as well as greater psychological well-being.

4. **Self-Monitoring**: Self-regulation involves ongoing self-monitoring and self-awareness, allowing individuals to assess their own thoughts, emotions, and behaviors in real-time. Self-monitoring involves keeping track of one's progress, identifying areas for improvement, and adjusting strategies as needed to stay on course. Self-monitoring is essential for maintaining self-control and adapting to changing circumstances.

5. **Goal Setting and Planning**: Self-regulation entails setting clear, achievable goals and developing plans to attain them. Goal setting provides direction and motivation, while planning involves breaking goals down into smaller, manageable steps and allocating resources effectively. Effective goal setting and planning enhance self-regulation by providing a roadmap for action and promoting accountability.

6. **Feedback and Adaptation**: Self-regulation involves seeking feedback from internal and external sources and using this information to adjust one's behavior and strategies as needed. Feedback allows individuals to monitor their progress, identify areas of strength and weakness, and make course corrections to stay on track toward their goals. Adaptability is a key aspect of self-regulation, enabling individuals to flexibly adjust their approach in response to changing circumstances and feedback.

Self-regulation is a multifaceted process that involves the coordination of cognitive, emotional, and behavioral skills to monitor, manage, and control one's thoughts, emotions, impulses, and behaviors. By developing self-regulation skills such as executive functions, emotional regulation, impulse control, self-monitoring, goal setting, and adaptability, individuals can enhance their ability to achieve goals, cope with stress, and lead fulfilling lives.

The Role of Emotional Control

Emotional control, also known as emotion regulation, is a critical aspect of self-regulation that plays a central role in psychological well-being, interpersonal relationships, and adaptive functioning. It involves the ability to monitor, evaluate, and modulate one's emotional responses in order to achieve desired outcomes, cope with stressors, and maintain emotional balance. Emotional control encompasses a range of cognitive, behavioral, and physiological processes aimed at effectively managing emotions in various situations.

Emotions are powerful internal experiences that influence thoughts, behaviors, and physiological arousal. While emotions serve important adaptive functions, such as signaling threats or opportunities, they can also become overwhelming or dysregulated, leading to negative outcomes. Emotional control allows individuals to respond to emotions in a constructive and adaptive manner, rather than being overwhelmed or reactive. It promotes psychological resilience, social competence, and overall well-being.

1. **Psychological Well-being**: Effective emotional control is associated with greater psychological well-being, including lower levels of anxiety, depression, and psychological distress. By regulating emotions, individuals can experience greater emotional stability, satisfaction with life, and overall happiness.
2. **Interpersonal Relationships**: Emotional control plays a crucial role in interpersonal relationships, as it enables individuals to navigate social interactions, communicate effectively, and resolve conflicts. By regulating emotions, individuals can express themselves assertively, empathize with others, and maintain positive relationships.
3. **Coping with Stress**: Emotion regulation helps individuals cope with stressors and adversity in a healthy and adaptive manner. By managing their emotional responses, individuals can reduce the impact of stress on their physical and mental health, leading to greater resilience and coping abilities.
4. **Decision-Making and Problem-Solving**: Emotional control enhances decision-making and problem-solving abilities by enabling individuals to think more clearly, consider alternative courses of action, and weigh the pros and cons of different options. By regulating emotions, individuals can make more rational, informed decisions that align with their goals and values.

Mechanisms of Emotional Control

Emotional control involves a complex interplay of

cognitive, behavioral, and physiological processes that influence the experience, expression, and regulation of emotions. Several key mechanisms underlie emotional control:

1. **Cognitive Reappraisal**: Cognitive reappraisal involves reframing the meaning of a situation in order to change one's emotional response. By altering how a situation is perceived or interpreted, individuals can modify their emotional reactions. For example, viewing a challenging task as an opportunity for growth rather than a threat can reduce feelings of anxiety and increase motivation.
2. **Expressive Suppression**: Expressive suppression involves inhibiting or suppressing the outward expression of emotions. While suppression may temporarily reduce the visible signs of emotion, it can also lead to increased physiological arousal and prolonged emotional distress. Expressive suppression is less effective than cognitive reappraisal for regulating emotions in the long term.
3. **Distraction and Attentional Deployment**: Distraction techniques involve redirecting attention away from emotional stimuli toward neutral or positive stimuli. By focusing on unrelated tasks or activities, individuals can temporarily reduce the intensity of their emotional responses. Attentional deployment strategies involve shifting attention toward or away from specific aspects of a situation in order to regulate emotions.
4. **Mindfulness and Acceptance**: Mindfulness involves nonjudgmental awareness of the present moment, including one's thoughts, feelings, and sensations. Mindfulness practices promote

acceptance of emotions as they arise, allowing individuals to observe and experience emotions without becoming overwhelmed or reactive. Mindfulness-based interventions have been shown to improve emotional regulation and psychological well-being.

Strategies for Enhancing Emotional Control

Enhancing emotional control requires the development of self-awareness, self-regulation skills, and adaptive coping strategies. Several strategies can help individuals improve their emotional control:

1. **Emotion Awareness**: Developing awareness of one's own emotions is the first step toward emotional control. Individuals can practice mindfulness and self-reflection to become more attuned to their emotional states, triggers, and patterns of reactivity.

2. **Cognitive Restructuring**: Cognitive restructuring involves identifying and challenging maladaptive thought patterns and beliefs that contribute to emotional distress. By replacing negative or irrational thoughts with more balanced and realistic ones, individuals can reduce the intensity of their emotional responses.

3. **Stress Management Techniques**: Engaging in stress management techniques such as deep breathing, progressive muscle relaxation, and guided imagery can help individuals reduce physiological arousal and promote emotional regulation. Regular exercise, adequate sleep, and healthy lifestyle habits also play a crucial role in managing stress and promoting emotional well-being.

4. **Social Support**: Seeking support from friends, family members, or mental health professionals

can provide validation, empathy, and perspective during times of emotional distress. Social support networks serve as a buffer against stress and can help individuals regulate their emotions more effectively.

5. **Emotion Regulation Training**: Participating in emotion regulation training programs or psychotherapy can teach individuals specific strategies for identifying, understanding, and regulating emotions. These programs often incorporate techniques such as cognitive restructuring, mindfulness, and problem-solving skills training.

Emotional control is a vital skill that influences psychological well-being, interpersonal relationships, and adaptive functioning. By effectively managing their emotions, individuals can cope with stressors, make informed decisions, and maintain emotional balance in various situations. Understanding the mechanisms of emotional control and implementing strategies for enhancing this skill can empower individuals to lead happier, healthier lives. Through self-awareness, self-regulation, and adaptive coping strategies, individuals can cultivate emotional resilience and thrive in the face of life's challenges.

Techniques for Self-Regulation

Self-regulation involves a variety of techniques aimed at monitoring, managing, and controlling one's thoughts, emotions, impulses, and behaviors. These techniques can be applied across different domains of life, including cognitive, emotional, and behavioral aspects. Here are some key techniques of self-regulation:

1. **Cognitive Reappraisal**: Cognitive reappraisal involves reframing the meaning of a situation in order to change one's emotional response. By

altering how a situation is perceived or interpreted, individuals can modify their emotional reactions. For example, viewing a challenging task as an opportunity for growth rather than a threat can reduce feelings of anxiety and increase motivation.

2. **Mindfulness Meditation**: Mindfulness meditation involves paying attention to the present moment with openness, curiosity, and acceptance. Practicing mindfulness cultivates self-awareness, emotional regulation, and mental clarity. By observing thoughts, emotions, and sensations as they arise, individuals develop a deeper understanding of their inner experiences and learn to respond more skillfully to life's challenges.

3. **Deep Breathing and Relaxation Techniques**: Deep breathing exercises, progressive muscle relaxation, and guided imagery are relaxation techniques that can help reduce physiological arousal and promote emotional regulation. These techniques activate the body's relaxation response, counteracting the stress response associated with emotional arousal.

4. **Attentional Control**: Attentional control techniques involve directing and maintaining attention on specific stimuli or tasks while inhibiting distractions. By focusing attention on relevant information and filtering out irrelevant stimuli, individuals can improve concentration, cognitive performance, and impulse control.

5. **Goal Setting and Planning**: Setting clear, achievable goals and developing plans to attain them is an important aspect of self-regulation. Goal setting provides direction and motivation, while planning involves breaking goals down into smaller, manageable steps and allocating

resources effectively. By setting SMART (Specific, Measurable, Achievable, Relevant, Time-bound) goals and creating action plans, individuals can enhance their self-regulation skills and achieve desired outcomes.

6. **Expressive Writing**: Expressive writing involves writing about one's thoughts, feelings, and experiences in a structured format. Writing about emotional experiences can help individuals process and make sense of their emotions, leading to increased self-awareness and emotional regulation. Expressive writing can also serve as a tool for problem-solving, stress reduction, and personal growth.
7. **Behavioral Activation**: Behavioral activation involves engaging in activities that promote positive emotions and well-being. By scheduling enjoyable and meaningful activities, individuals can increase positive reinforcement and reduce negative reinforcement, leading to improved mood and motivation. Behavioral activation can also help individuals overcome avoidance behaviors and increase engagement in valued activities.
8. **Social Support and Coping Strategies**: Seeking support from friends, family members, or mental health professionals can provide validation, empathy, and perspective during times of emotional distress. Social support networks serve as a buffer against stress and can help individuals regulate their emotions more effectively. Coping strategies such as problem-solving, seeking information, and seeking emotional support can also enhance self-regulation skills and promote resilience.
9. **Biofeedback and Self-Monitoring**: Biofeedback techniques involve using electronic monitoring

devices to provide real-time feedback on physiological responses such as heart rate, breathing rate, and muscle tension. By monitoring their physiological responses, individuals can learn to recognize signs of stress or emotional arousal and develop strategies for self-regulation. Self-monitoring techniques, such as keeping a mood diary or using smartphone apps, can also help individuals track their emotions, behaviors, and progress toward goals.

10. **Cognitive Restructuring**: Cognitive restructuring involves identifying and challenging maladaptive thought patterns and beliefs that contribute to emotional distress. By replacing negative or irrational thoughts with more balanced and realistic ones, individuals can reduce the intensity of their emotional responses and improve their overall well-being.

Self-regulation techniques encompass a variety of cognitive, emotional, and behavioral strategies aimed at monitoring, managing, and controlling one's thoughts, emotions, impulses, and behaviors. By practicing these techniques regularly and incorporating them into daily life, individuals can enhance their self-regulation skills and promote psychological resilience, emotional well-being, and personal growth.

Cognitive Reframing

Cognitive reframing, also known as cognitive restructuring or cognitive reappraisal, is a powerful technique used in cognitive-behavioral therapy (CBT) and other therapeutic approaches to help individuals change their perspective on a situation, event, or thought pattern. It involves identifying and challenging maladaptive or negative thought patterns and replacing them with more balanced, realistic, and adaptive interpretations. Cognitive reframing is based on the premise that the way individuals interpret events influences their emotional reactions, behaviors, and overall well-being. By changing their cognitive interpretations, individuals can alter their emotional responses, improve their coping abilities, and enhance their overall quality of life.

Understanding Cognitive Reframing

Cognitive reframing is grounded in the cognitive model of psychopathology, which posits that psychological distress is often caused or exacerbated by dysfunctional thought patterns or cognitive distortions. These distortions can include all-or-nothing thinking, catastrophizing, personalization, overgeneralization, and other irrational beliefs. Cognitive reframing aims to challenge and modify these distorted thoughts by encouraging individuals to examine the evidence, consider alternative explanations, and generate more balanced interpretations.

The process of cognitive reframing typically involves several steps:

1. **Identifying Distorted Thoughts**: The first step in cognitive reframing is to identify and become aware of maladaptive or negative thought patterns. This may involve paying attention to automatic thoughts that arise in response to specific situations or triggers. Common cognitive distortions include black-and-white thinking, jumping to conclusions, and discounting the positive.

2. **Challenging Negative Beliefs**: Once distorted thoughts have been identified, individuals can begin to challenge and evaluate their validity. This may involve questioning the evidence supporting the negative beliefs, examining alternative explanations, and considering the potential consequences of maintaining these beliefs.

Techniques such as Socratic questioning, reality testing, and behavioral experiments can be helpful in this process.

3. **Generating Alternative Interpretations**: After challenging negative beliefs, individuals can work to generate more balanced, realistic, and adaptive interpretations of the situation. This may involve reframing the situation in a more positive light, considering alternative perspectives, or focusing on aspects of the situation that are within their control. By shifting their perspective, individuals can reduce the intensity of their emotional reactions and improve their ability to cope with challenges.
4. **Testing New Interpretations**: Finally, individuals can test their new interpretations in real-life situations to see how they affect their emotional responses and behaviors. This may involve intentionally exposing themselves to situations that typically trigger negative thoughts and observing how their reactions change based on their new perspective. Through repeated practice and reinforcement, individuals can solidify their new cognitive patterns and build resilience against future challenges.

Benefits of Cognitive Reframing

Cognitive reframing offers a range of benefits for emotional well-being, psychological resilience, and overall quality of life:

1. **Reduced Emotional Distress**: By challenging negative thought patterns and adopting more balanced interpretations, individuals can reduce the intensity of their emotional responses to stressful or challenging situations. Cognitive reframing helps individuals gain perspective,

reframe catastrophic thinking, and cultivate greater emotional resilience.

2. **Improved Coping Skills**: Cognitive reframing enhances individuals' ability to cope with adversity and uncertainty by promoting adaptive coping strategies. By changing their cognitive interpretations, individuals can develop more effective problem-solving skills, enhance their coping resources, and build confidence in their ability to overcome challenges.
3. **Enhanced Decision-Making**: Cognitive reframing enables individuals to make more informed and rational decisions by reducing cognitive biases and distortions. By considering alternative perspectives and weighing the evidence objectively, individuals can make decisions that are aligned with their values, goals, and priorities.
4. **Increased Self-Confidence**: Cognitive reframing promotes a sense of self-efficacy and empowerment by highlighting individuals' ability to change their thoughts and perceptions. By challenging negative beliefs and generating more adaptive interpretations, individuals can build confidence in their ability to cope with adversity and achieve their goals.
5. **Improved Interpersonal Relationships**: Cognitive reframing can enhance interpersonal relationships by promoting empathy, understanding, and communication. By reframing negative interpretations of others' behavior, individuals can reduce conflict, improve communication, and strengthen their relationships with others.
6. **Enhanced Overall Well-Being**: Ultimately, cognitive reframing contributes to greater overall

well-being by fostering a more positive outlook on life, promoting psychological flexibility, and reducing the impact of stressors on mental health. By changing their cognitive interpretations, individuals can cultivate greater emotional resilience, satisfaction with life, and a sense of meaning and purpose.

Applications of Cognitive Reframing

Cognitive reframing techniques are widely used in various therapeutic settings, including cognitive-behavioral therapy (CBT), acceptance and commitment therapy (ACT), dialectical behavior therapy (DBT), and positive psychology interventions. These techniques can be applied to a wide range of psychological issues, including anxiety, depression, stress, trauma, and relationship problems. Cognitive reframing can also be used in everyday life to enhance resilience, improve coping skills, and promote emotional well-being.

Cognitive reframing is a valuable technique for promoting emotional regulation, enhancing coping skills, and improving overall well-being. By challenging negative thought patterns and adopting more balanced interpretations, individuals can reduce emotional distress, improve decision-making, and build resilience in the face of life's challenges. Through practice and repetition, cognitive reframing can become a powerful tool for promoting psychological resilience, enhancing self-confidence, and fostering a more positive outlook on life.

Stress Management Techniques

Stress management techniques are strategies and practices aimed at reducing, coping with, or preventing the negative effects of stress on physical, emotional, and psychological well-being. These techniques are essential for maintaining health, enhancing resilience, and promoting overall quality of life in the face of various stressors. Stress management techniques encompass a wide range of approaches, including cognitive-behavioral strategies, relaxation techniques, lifestyle modifications, and social support interventions. Here are some effective stress management techniques:

1. **Cognitive-Behavioral Techniques:**
   - **Cognitive Restructuring**: Cognitive restructuring involves identifying and challenging negative or irrational thoughts associated with stressors. By replacing distorted thoughts with more balanced and realistic ones, individuals can reduce the intensity of their emotional reactions to stressors.
   - **Problem-Solving Skills Training**: Problem-solving skills training helps individuals identify stressors, generate alternative solutions, and implement effective problem-solving strategies. By developing problem-solving skills, individuals can address stressors more effectively and reduce feelings of helplessness or overwhelm.
   - **Assertiveness Training**: Assertiveness training teaches individuals how to express their needs, preferences, and boundaries in a clear, direct, and respectful manner. By asserting themselves effectively, individuals can reduce interpersonal conflict, enhance communication skills, and manage stressors related to social interactions.
   - **Time Management**: Time management techniques help individuals prioritize tasks, set realistic goals, and allocate time effectively. By organizing their time and resources, individuals

can reduce feelings of overwhelm, increase productivity, and improve work-life balance.

2. **Relaxation Techniques:**
   - **Deep Breathing**: Deep breathing exercises, such as diaphragmatic breathing or belly breathing, involve taking slow, deep breaths to activate the body's relaxation response. Deep breathing can reduce physiological arousal, lower heart rate, and promote feelings of calmness and relaxation.
   - **Progressive Muscle Relaxation (PMR)**: PMR involves systematically tensing and relaxing different muscle groups in the body to reduce tension and promote relaxation. By practicing PMR regularly, individuals can increase awareness of muscle tension and learn to release tension more effectively.
   - **Guided Imagery**: Guided imagery involves visualizing peaceful, calming, or pleasant scenes to evoke relaxation and reduce stress. Guided imagery scripts may guide individuals through imaginary journeys to natural settings, peaceful landscapes, or comforting environments.
   - **Mindfulness Meditation**: Mindfulness meditation involves paying attention to the present moment with openness, curiosity, and acceptance. By cultivating mindfulness skills, individuals can increase self-awareness, reduce rumination, and develop a nonjudgmental attitude toward their thoughts and emotions.
3. **Lifestyle Modifications:**
   - **Regular Exercise**: Regular physical activity,

such as walking, jogging, swimming, or yoga, can help reduce stress by promoting the release of endorphins, improving mood, and reducing muscle tension. Exercise also provides an outlet for pent-up energy and stress.

- **Healthy Eating Habits**: A balanced diet rich in fruits, vegetables, whole grains, lean proteins, and healthy fats can support overall health and resilience to stress. Avoiding excessive caffeine, alcohol, and processed foods can also help regulate mood and energy levels.
- **Adequate Sleep**: Prioritizing adequate sleep is essential for managing stress and promoting overall well-being. Poor sleep can exacerbate stress, impair cognitive function, and weaken the body's ability to cope with stressors. Establishing a consistent sleep schedule and practicing good sleep hygiene can improve sleep quality and resilience to stress.
- **Relaxing Activities**: Engaging in hobbies, interests, or activities that bring joy, relaxation, and fulfillment can help reduce stress and promote emotional well-being. Whether it's reading, gardening, painting, or listening to music, finding time for relaxation and leisure activities is essential for managing stress.

4. **Social Support Interventions:**

- **Seeking Support**: Seeking support from friends, family members, or mental health professionals can provide validation, empathy, and perspective during times of stress. Social support networks serve as a buffer against stress and can help individuals cope more effectively with stressors.
- **Joining Support Groups**: Joining support

groups or peer-led communities can provide a sense of belonging, understanding, and camaraderie. Support groups offer opportunities for individuals to share experiences, gain insights, and learn coping strategies from others facing similar challenges.

Stress management techniques encompass a variety of cognitive-behavioral strategies, relaxation techniques, lifestyle modifications, and social support interventions aimed at reducing, coping with, or preventing the negative effects of stress. By incorporating these techniques into their daily lives, individuals can enhance their resilience, improve their coping abilities, and promote overall well-being in the face of stressors.

Developing Impulse Control

Developing impulse control is a crucial aspect of self-regulation that enables individuals to resist immediate gratification, delay impulsive reactions, and make thoughtful, deliberate choices aligned with their long-term goals and values. Impulse control involves the ability to regulate one's impulses, urges, and desires in order to achieve desired outcomes and maintain self-discipline. Developing impulse control requires self-awareness, self-regulation skills, and practice in managing impulses across different domains of life. Here are some key strategies for developing impulse control:

1. **Self-Awareness:**
    - Developing impulse control begins with self-awareness, or the ability to recognize and monitor one's thoughts, emotions, and behaviors. By becoming more aware of their impulses and triggers, individuals can better understand the underlying motivations driving their actions.
    - Self-awareness involves paying attention to

internal cues, such as physical sensations, emotions, and urges, as well as external triggers, such as environmental stimuli or social pressures. Mindfulness practices, such as meditation or reflective journaling, can help individuals cultivate greater self-awareness and insight into their impulses.

2. **Understanding Impulses:**
    - Understanding the nature of impulses is essential for developing impulse control. Impulses are automatic, often subconscious urges to act in a certain way in response to internal or external stimuli. They can be driven by emotions, habits, biological factors, or environmental cues.
    - Recognizing the difference between healthy impulses, such as hunger or thirst, and unhealthy impulses, such as addictive behaviors or impulsive spending, is important for developing impulse control. Understanding the consequences of acting on impulsive urges can help individuals make more informed decisions about how to respond.
3. **Delaying Gratification:**
    - Delaying gratification is a key component of impulse control that involves resisting the temptation for immediate rewards in favor of long-term goals or values. Developing the ability to delay gratification requires patience, self-discipline, and the willingness to tolerate discomfort or uncertainty in the short term for greater rewards in the future.
    - Techniques such as setting goals, creating action plans, and establishing rewards systems can help individuals stay motivated and

focused on their long-term objectives. Breaking goals down into smaller, more manageable steps can make them less overwhelming and easier to achieve over time.

4. **Practicing Self-Regulation:**

   - Self-regulation skills are essential for managing impulses and maintaining self-control. Self-regulation involves monitoring, evaluating, and modulating one's thoughts, emotions, and behaviors in order to achieve desired outcomes. It requires the ability to regulate attention, inhibit impulsive responses, and engage in goal-directed behavior.

   - Techniques such as cognitive reappraisal, emotion regulation, and problem-solving can help individuals regulate their thoughts and emotions in order to resist impulsive urges. Building self-regulation skills through practice and repetition strengthens the neural circuits involved in impulse control and enhances self-discipline over time.

5. **Developing Coping Strategies:**

   - Developing coping strategies for managing stress, boredom, or other triggers for impulsive behavior can help individuals reduce the likelihood of acting on impulsive urges. Coping strategies may include relaxation techniques, such as deep breathing or progressive muscle relaxation, or engaging in alternative activities, such as exercise or creative pursuits.

   - Identifying healthy outlets for stress or emotional distress, such as talking to a friend, seeking professional support, or engaging in hobbies or interests, can provide individuals with constructive ways to cope with difficult emotions without resorting to impulsive behavior.

6. **Seeking Support and Accountability:**
   - Seeking support from friends, family members, or mental health professionals can provide encouragement, guidance, and accountability in developing impulse control. Social support networks can offer validation, empathy, and practical assistance in overcoming challenges and staying on track toward goals.
   - Accountability partners or support groups can provide motivation and accountability by setting goals, tracking progress, and celebrating achievements together. Knowing that others are rooting for their success can boost individuals' confidence and commitment to developing impulse control.

Developing impulse control is a gradual process that involves self-awareness, self-regulation skills, and practice in managing impulses effectively. By understanding their impulses, delaying gratification, practicing self-regulation, developing coping strategies, and seeking support, individuals can strengthen their ability to resist impulsive urges and make more intentional choices aligned with their long-term goals and values. Through consistent effort and perseverance, developing impulse control can lead to greater self-discipline, resilience, and personal growth.

3

Motivation

Motivation is a fundamental aspect of human behavior, driving individuals to pursue goals, overcome obstacles, and achieve desired outcomes. It plays a central role in shaping thoughts, emotions, and behaviors, influencing everything from academic performance and career success to personal relationships and health habits. Understanding motivation is essential for unlocking human potential, promoting well-being, and facilitating personal and professional growth. In this introduction, we will explore the nature of motivation, its underlying theories, and its impact on various aspects of life.

At its core, motivation refers to the processes that initiate, guide, and sustain goal-directed behavior. It involves the interplay of internal and external factors that energize, direct, and regulate behavior toward specific objectives. Motivation encompasses a wide range of psychological processes, including goal setting, goal pursuit, self-regulation, and reinforcement.

Motivation can be influenced by various factors, including individual differences, environmental cues, and situational contexts. It can be driven by intrinsic factors, such as personal interests, values, and aspirations, or extrinsic factors, such as rewards, punishments, and social expectations. Motivation can also vary in intensity, fluctuating in response to changes in internal states, external stimuli, or the perceived significance of goals.

Motivation is a complex psychological concept that refers to the processes that initiate, guide, and sustain goal-directed behavior. It involves the interplay of internal and external factors that energize, direct, and regulate behavior toward specific objectives. Motivation encompasses a wide range of cognitive, emotional, and physiological processes that influence individuals' thoughts, attitudes, and actions.

At its core, motivation involves the activation of goal-relevant processes that drive individuals to pursue desired outcomes, overcome obstacles, and achieve personal or organizational goals. Motivation can be intrinsic, arising from internal desires, interests, and values, or extrinsic, driven by external rewards, punishments, or social pressures.

The concept of motivation encompasses several key components:

1. **Activation**: Motivation involves the initiation or activation of goal-directed behavior, often in response to internal needs, desires, or external stimuli. Activation refers to the arousal of cognitive, emotional, and physiological processes that energize and mobilize individuals to take action.
2. **Direction**: Motivation provides direction and guidance for behavior by orienting individuals

toward specific goals, objectives, or outcomes. Directionality involves setting priorities, making choices, and allocating resources in ways that align with one's goals and values.

3. **Intensity**: Motivation varies in intensity, ranging from low to high levels of arousal or engagement. The intensity of motivation reflects the degree of effort, persistence, and commitment individuals invest in pursuing their goals or tasks.
4. **Persistence**: Motivation influences individuals' ability to persist in the face of obstacles, setbacks, or challenges. Persistent motivation involves maintaining focus, effort, and resilience in pursuit of goals, even when faced with difficulties or delays.
5. **Satisfaction**: Motivation is often accompanied by feelings of satisfaction, fulfillment, or achievement upon reaching goals or attaining desired outcomes. Satisfaction serves as a reward for successful goal attainment and reinforces future motivation.

Motivation can be influenced by various factors, including individual differences, environmental cues, social norms, and situational contexts. It can arise from intrinsic sources, such as personal interests, values, and aspirations, or extrinsic sources, such as rewards, punishments, or social approval. Motivation can also be shaped by cognitive processes, such as goal setting, self-efficacy beliefs, and expectancy-value appraisals, as well as emotional processes, such as mood, arousal, and affective states.

Overall, motivation is a dynamic and multifaceted phenomenon that plays a central role in shaping human behavior, cognition, and emotion.

Theories of Motivation

Numerous theories have been proposed to explain

the nature and dynamics of motivation, each offering unique insights into the underlying mechanisms driving behavior. Some of the most influential theories of motivation include:

1. **Maslow's Hierarchy of Needs**: Abraham Maslow's theory posits that human motivation is shaped by a hierarchy of needs, ranging from basic physiological needs, such as food and shelter, to higher-level needs, such as self-esteem and self-actualization. According to Maslow, individuals are motivated to fulfill lower-level needs before progressing to higher-level needs.
2. **Herzberg's Two-Factor Theory**: Frederick Herzberg's theory distinguishes between hygiene factors, which are external factors that can cause dissatisfaction if absent (e.g., salary, working conditions), and motivators, which are internal factors that can lead to job satisfaction and motivation (e.g., recognition, responsibility).
3. **Expectancy Theory**: Victor Vroom's expectancy theory proposes that individuals are motivated to act in certain ways based on their expectations of desired outcomes and the perceived likelihood of achieving those outcomes. According to this theory, motivation is influenced by three factors: expectancy (belief that effort will lead to performance), instrumentality (belief that performance will lead to rewards), and valence (value attached to rewards).
4. **Self-Determination Theory (SDT)**: Self-determination theory posits that individuals are inherently motivated to satisfy three basic psychological needs: autonomy (sense of control and choice), competence (sense of mastery and effectiveness), and relatedness (sense of connection and belonging). According to SDT,

intrinsic motivation, which arises from the fulfillment of these needs, is more sustainable and satisfying than extrinsic motivation.

5. **Goal-Setting Theory**: Edwin Locke and Gary Latham's goal-setting theory emphasizes the importance of setting specific, challenging goals in motivating behavior. According to this theory, clear goals provide direction, focus attention, and enhance performance by mobilizing effort and persistence.

The Impact of Motivation

Motivation influences virtually every aspect of human behavior, cognition, and emotion, shaping individuals' thoughts, attitudes, and actions in profound ways. The impact of motivation extends across various domains of life, including:

1. **Academic Achievement**: Motivation plays a critical role in academic success, influencing students' engagement, effort, and persistence in learning tasks. Motivated students are more likely to set goals, seek challenges, and adopt effective learning strategies, leading to higher academic performance and achievement.
2. **Career Success**: Motivation is essential for career development and success, driving individuals to pursue challenging goals, develop skills, and advance in their professions. Motivated employees are more productive, innovative, and satisfied with their work, contributing to organizational success and competitiveness.
3. **Health and Well-being**: Motivation affects health behaviors and outcomes, influencing individuals' adherence to healthy habits, such as exercise, diet, and stress management. Motivated individuals are more likely to adopt health-promoting behaviors, seek medical care, and

adhere to treatment regimens, leading to better physical and mental health outcomes.

4. **Relationships and Interpersonal Dynamics**: Motivation shapes interpersonal relationships and social interactions, influencing individuals' attitudes, communication styles, and behaviors in social contexts. Motivated individuals are more likely to invest time and effort in building and maintaining relationships, fostering trust, intimacy, and mutual support.
5. **Personal Growth and Fulfillment**: Motivation is essential for personal growth and fulfillment, driving individuals to pursue meaningful goals, develop skills, and realize their potential. Motivated individuals are more resilient in the face of challenges, more adaptable to change, and more likely to experience a sense of purpose and satisfaction in life.

Motivation is a multifaceted phenomenon that plays a central role in human behavior, cognition, and emotion. Understanding the nature of motivation, its underlying theories, and its impact on various aspects of life is essential for promoting well-being, facilitating personal and professional growth, and unlocking human potential. By recognizing the factors that influence motivation and employing effective strategies for enhancing motivation, individuals can achieve their goals, overcome obstacles, and lead fulfilling lives.

Understanding Different Types of Motivation

Motivation can be defined as a reason (or reasons) which leads an individual to act in a certain way. The phenomenon of motivation is not limited to just humans, and occurs in every organism living. The reasons might not always be the same between two individuals acting in a certain way, but almost every action is directed by certain motivation.

Motivation can be further divided into two different types:

1. Intrinsic Motivation
2. Extrinsic Motivation

Intrinsic Motivation

It is a form of motivation in which the impetus originates internally within the organism. It denotes the internal motivating force that compels an individual to exhibit a particular course of action. It consists of all physiological drives, including but not limited to appetite, thirst, sleep, pain relief, temperature regulation, and oxygen necessity.

Intrinsic motivation encompasses all activities that inspire you through internal rewards, such as assisting a companion in need or striving for personal growth. One possible reason for one's motivation to obtain a promotion is the acquisition of advantageous skills. You may, conversely, be driven to achieve success due to your desire to make a positive impact on the lives of those in your vicinity.

Despite the positive examples provided above, intrinsic motivation can also be motivated by negative factors. For instance, we can inspire ourselves to acquire new knowledge by the knowledge that failure to do so will result in a sense of dissatisfaction. While our actions did produce a positive result, the motivation we employed was preoccupied with preventing a negative consequence rather than generating a positive one. There are numerous varieties of intrinsic motivation, each of which is predicated on a distinct incentive or motivator.

Irrespective of their nature, intrinsic motivation is generally more enduring than extrinsic motivation due to its tendency to concentrate on attainable positive or altruistic outcomes. In contrast, extrinsic motivation generally pertains to external rewards and desires, which are thus not directly under one's volition to attain.

Intrinsic motivation is defined as the doing of an activity for its inherent satisfaction rather than for some separable consequence.

According to **Lawler**, "intrinsic motivation is the degree to which feelings of esteem, growth, and competence are expected to result from successful task performance".

According to **Porter**, "intrinsic motivation to an expectancy approach and expectancy theory which clearly indicates that intrinsic and extrinsic motivations summate".

It includes the following motives:

- **Biological drives**
- **Curiosity**
- **Internal fears**
- **Psychological needs**
- **Internal desires**

Extrinsic Motivation

Motives of this nature originate from sources external to the human body. The propelling force, which motivates an individual to perform specific actions, is external to the human body. Although these motivations are not intrinsic to the human body, they can still have either a beneficial or detrimental effect on the individual.

Extrinsic motivation comprises all forms of encouragement derived from external rewards, such as monetary compensation or commendation. The aforementioned motivational styles, which are contingent upon extrinsic factors such as fear, expectation, or tangible incentives, are more prevalent than intrinsic motivators. For instance, individuals desire a promotion due to the anticipated salary increase.

External motivation, similar to intrinsic motivation, can occasionally have adverse effects. An instance of psychological motivation could be the apprehension of termination from one's job. This demonstrates that, similar to its higher-level counterpart, extrinsic motivation encompasses a variety of motivational categories, each of which emphasizes a distinct external motivational driver and explains its effectiveness as a motivator. Evidently, motivation defies a straightforward classification as either an intrinsic or extrinsic incentive.

It includes the following motives:

- **Incentives**
- **Bonuses**
- **Allowances**
- **Promotion and Demotion**
- **Rewards and Punishment**
- **Merit and Distinction Certificates**
- **Appreciation Certificates and Prizes**

Differences between Intrinsic Motivation and Extrinsic Motivation

Intrinsic Motivation	Extrinsic Motivation
The act of being motivated by internal factors to perform certain actions and behavior is called *Intrinsic Motivation.*	Whenever an individual performs an action or behavior because the individual is affected by the eternal factors such as rewards or punishments, such form of motivation is called *Extrinsic Motivation.*
There is neither pressure nor any sort of reward for the actions you perform due to intrinsic motivation.	You get rewarded as promised for the actions you perform due to extrinsic motivation.
The needs or causes that lead to intrinsic motivation are: • Autonomy: the need to have complete control over one's own life. • Relatedness: the need to maintain companionship or connection with others.	The needs or causes that lead to extrinsic motivation (and not limited to) are: • Money • Praise • Competition • Threat of a punishment

• Competence: the need to do be the best and/or succeed.	
Intrinsic incentives are hard to figure. In a class or workplace, different individuals will/might require different approaches.	Extrinsic incentives can be used to motivate a whole group, thus increasing productivity in workplace or creating a better learning environment in classrooms.
Fostering intrinsic motivation can be a lengthy process, requiring special treatment.	Extrinsic Motivation often occur instantly as soon as the subject understands the perks of performing certain actions.
Intrinsic Motivation lasts for longer periods and often leads to higher level of success.	Extrinsic Motivation might only occur for limited period of time, and the individual stops performing actions after the punishment or reward is applied.
Example 1: A student attends guitar classes because he wanted to. Whether he was inspired by some rockstars or just enjoyed the idea of playing in front of a crowd, this sort of motivation is classified as intrinsic motivation. In the above example, there is a higher chance for a student to carry on playing guitar and reach stardom in the years to come.	Example 1: A student attends guitar classes because his parents promise to double his allowance money. In the above example, the chances of the student learning guitar efficiently is quite low, as the student only seeks an excuse to quit. Additionally, the student is most likely to give up playing guitar if the allowance money isn't doubled as promised.
Example 2: A group of students might not all get intrinsically motivated, which could hamper class productivity.	Example 2: A group of students could be persuaded with the promise of rewards, or even motivated under the fear of punishment. Regardless of the matter of motivation, the whole class would perform well increasing the overall productivity.

Other types of Motivation

The following are the types of motivation:

1. **Positive Motivation:** Incentives or positive motivation are founded upon the provision of rewards. Incentive schemes are implemented to motivate the workforce to attain the intended objectives. The incentives could manifest as various forms such as increased compensation, career advancement, acknowledgment of efforts, and so forth. Upon being presented with the incentives, the employees voluntarily strive to enhance their performance. Peter Drucker posits that genuine and constructive motivators comprise worker placement, a high performance standard, sufficient information for self-control, and active worker participation as a responsible member of the plant community. Positive motivation is generated when employees collaborate and experience a sense of joy.
2. **Negative Motivation:** Negative or fear-based motivation stems from coercion or dread. The actions of employees are influenced by fear. If they fail to conduct themselves appropriately, they could face repercussions such as demotions or terminations. Fear functions as an incentive mechanism. The employees cooperate against their will, as opposed to voluntarily, in order to evade punishment. Employees may achieve a level of performance where punishment is not an option, but this type of motivation elicits feelings of wrath and frustration. This form of motivation typically culminates in labor disputes. Despite the inherent limitations of negative motivation, it remains a prevalent approach for attaining intended outcomes. It may be difficult to find management that has not, at some point, implemented negative motivation.

3. **Competence & Learning Motivation:** Competence motivation, alternatively referred to as learning motivation, posits that individuals are more intrinsically motivated by the learning process than by the ultimate reward. Competence motivation is distinguished by the fact that individuals are literally motivated by the process of learning or improving themselves as they approach the fulfillment of a goal or task, rather than by the end result. Motivation based on competence or learning occurs, for instance, when an individual desires a promotion for the purpose of acquiring valuable skills rather than the anticipated salary increase. This is a highly effective motivator that ought to be incorporated into virtually every motivational strategy. For this reason, fresh, pertinent competencies are frequently more valuable than monetary compensation, as they are intangible assets that are impervious to tampering.

4. **Attitude Motivation:** Attitude motivation pertains to the form of motivation fostered by the aspiration to alter one's own or others' thoughts and emotions. Although there are certain parallels to the externally-oriented social motivation discussed later, attitude-driven motivation is characterized by individuals engaging in behaviors and interactions with the explicit intention of positively and upliftingly affecting themselves and others. Motivation by a change in attitude could include, for instance, working for a non-profit organization or volunteering at a charity kitchen because it makes you feel good to make others feel good. A manager who derives satisfaction from fostering the development and achievement of their direct reports is also engaging in attitude motivation.

5. **Achievement Motivation:** Individuals are achievement motivated when they have the desire to pursue and accomplish particular objectives. Individuals who are propelled by this form of motivation are not necessarily motivated by the associated reward, but rather by the accomplishment of the task or objective in and of itself. An entrepreneur may establish a company, for instance, with the intention of constructing a world-class organization, and not necessarily for financial gain. Individuals who are motivated by achievement tend to be self-motivated and process-oriented, placing greater importance on the improvement process rather than the final product. Although the accomplishment of a target may appear to be an extrinsic incentive, this form of motivation is predominantly internal in nature. The reason for this is that the sense of achievement one receives upon accomplishing a deserving task is more appealing than the flash and grandeur of monetary rewards.

6. **Creative Motivation:** Numerous individuals are driven by creativity or an intrinsic desire to convey themselves creatively. One enters a state of creative motivation when the desire to convey oneself serves as a motivating factor. Examples of creative motivation include things in which you feel compelled to create, such as the motivation to write a book, act in a movie, play the guitar, build a product, or start a business. Creative motivation generally takes the form of an intrinsic conviction that one possesses a message that requires expression. Regardless of the intended audience (the entire world or a select few), any artistic creation undertaken for the purpose of self-expression is propelled by creative inspiration. Although one's creations may have a physical form, they may also be immaterial or transient.

7. **Physiological Motivation:** The motivations of humans are frequently irrational internal forces. For instance, this may occur when an individual pursues another individual out of affection. Regardless of our best efforts, your actions are driven by primordial physiological sensations that are profound and cannot be disregarded. This comprises the internal and external physiological motivational factors that we cannot influence. Take into account Maslow's Hierarchy of Needs. In addition to fundamental needs like food and shelter, all humans are driven by higher-level psychological needs and the pursuit of self-actualization. These needs are intrinsic to every individual and serve as internal motivators to attain them regardless of the consequences; this knowledge is beneficial when attempting to comprehend one's own or others' thought processes.
8. **Incentive Motivation:** In contrast to achievement motivation, incentive motivation posits that individuals are more motivated by the reward received rather than by the actual accomplishment of the objective. Rather than being driven by the pursuance of a task, incentive-motivated individuals are compelled to act in anticipation of a specific (and frequently anticipated) reward. An illustration of this would be prioritizing a higher salary over the fulfillment derived from a new responsibility when seeking a promotion; such an individual would be motivated by incentives rather than achievement. Despite this, incentive motivation is not entirely negative. Although it may appear to be the antithesis of achievement motivation, the two can be utilized in tandem. For instance, one may find motivation in a promotion through the combination of a

higher salary and more challenging yet gratifying tasks. This situation is mutually beneficial, as both parties receive external rewards and experience internal satisfaction. Determine which objectives or undertakings include both incentives and elements of achievement motivation.

9. **Fear Motivation:** Fear motivation is a form of motivation that employs repercussions to stimulate behavior. One could consider fear motivation a "negative motivator" because it is characterized by the avoidance of suffering or consequences rather than a reward. Fear motivation employs punishment or negative motivators—such as termination—instead of positive incentives to encourage individuals or groups to progress productively toward particular objectives, tasks, or deliverables. Although fear motivation may seem detrimental, it can in fact serve as a beneficial force. For instance, one may strategize a summer pool party at their residence or apartment complex and employ the apprehension of appearing unfit as an incentive to adhere to a fitness regimen and dietary regimen. Consider fear motivation to be constructive constraints or positive stressors that assist you in outsmarting your future self, conquering negative habits, and living the life you desire (but were previously too afraid to pursue).

10. **Power Motivation:** According to the power motivational factor, individuals are driven by the desire for authority and influence over their own lives as well as the lives of others. Individuals are frequently motivated to increase their overall life options and exert control over their surroundings because they desire options. As a consequence, power motivation becomes evident in the aspiration to exert influence over our own lives

as well as the lives of those in our vicinity. Instances of power motivation at its most extreme can be observed in historical atrocities such as Nazi Germany and others where the desire to exert control over others surpasses any moral duty or code. Nevertheless, power motivation can have a positive impact when reduced. For instance, while attempting to exert control over others may be undesirable, doing so over one's own life can be beneficial. Thus, power motivation inspires you to manifest the life you desire through deliberate thought and action.

11. **Affiliation & Social Motivation:** Social motivation, which is also referred to as affiliation motivation, posits that individuals are driven by social constructs such as acceptability and a sense of belonging. Humans possess an intrinsic yearning for interpersonal connection, and social motivation compels us to pursue such connections through participation in a social collective. Although it may appear to be internally motivating, acceptance is frequently the driving force and cannot be bestowed upon oneself in a group setting. According to evolutionary psychology, these social factors motivate every human being. It is therefore essential to continually cultivate the relationships you already have and search out new ones. Discovering a community of individuals who accept and adore you can inspire you to achieve greater heights and lead to genuine happiness.

The Role of Motivation in Emotional Intelligence

The role of motivation in emotional intelligence (EI) is significant, as it influences individuals' ability to recognize, understand, and manage emotions in themselves and others. Motivation serves as a driving force behind EI competencies, shaping individuals' attitudes, goals, and behaviors in ways that promote emotional well-being, interpersonal relationships, and personal growth.

The role of motivation in emotional intelligence (EI) is fundamental, as it serves as a driving force behind individuals' ability to recognize, understand, and manage emotions in themselves and others. Motivation influences various aspects of emotional intelligence, shaping individuals' attitudes, goals, and behaviors in ways that promote emotional well-being, interpersonal relationships, and personal growth.

1. **Intrinsic Motivation and Self-Awareness:** Intrinsic motivation, driven by internal factors such as curiosity, passion, or personal interest, plays a crucial role in the development of self-awareness, a foundational component of emotional intelligence. Individuals who are intrinsically motivated to explore their emotions, values, and beliefs are more likely to engage in self-reflection, introspection, and introspective activities that deepen their understanding of themselves. For example, someone who is intrinsically motivated to improve their emotional intelligence may regularly journal about their thoughts and feelings, seek feedback from others, or participate in self-discovery exercises. Their intrinsic motivation to learn and grow emotionally fuels their self-awareness efforts, leading to greater insight into their emotions, strengths, and areas for development.
2. **Extrinsic Motivation and Social Awareness:** Extrinsic motivation, driven by external rewards or incentives, can also influence individuals' social awareness, another key component of emotional intelligence. Social awareness involves recognizing

and understanding the emotions, needs, and perspectives of others, which is essential for effective communication, empathy, and interpersonal relationships. For instance, individuals who are extrinsically motivated by the desire for social approval or recognition may be more attuned to others' emotions and social cues in order to navigate social interactions successfully. Their extrinsic motivation to gain approval or avoid rejection encourages them to pay attention to others' emotions and adjust their behavior accordingly, thereby enhancing their social awareness skills.

3. **Achievement Motivation and Self-Management:** Achievement motivation, the desire to excel, succeed, and accomplish challenging goals, plays a significant role in self-management, another key aspect of emotional intelligence. Self-management involves regulating one's emotions, impulses, and behaviors in ways that promote personal and interpersonal effectiveness. Individuals with high levels of achievement motivation are motivated to set and pursue ambitious goals, overcome obstacles, and persevere in the face of setbacks, all of which are essential for effective self-management. Their drive to achieve success and accomplish their goals provides the energy and focus needed to manage stress, control impulses, and maintain emotional balance, even in challenging situations.

4. **Social Motivation and Relationship Management:** Social motivation, the desire to connect with others, build relationships, and gain acceptance or approval from social groups, plays a crucial role in relationship management, the final component of emotional intelligence. Relationship management involves effectively

managing interpersonal interactions, resolving conflicts, and building strong, positive relationships with others. Individuals who are socially motivated are more likely to invest time and effort in developing and maintaining relationships, as they value social connections and the benefits they provide. Their social motivation drives them to communicate openly, show empathy, and collaborate effectively with others, leading to more fulfilling and harmonious relationships.

5. **Motivation and Emotional Regulation:** Motivation also plays a key role in emotional regulation, the process of managing and modulating one's emotions in response to internal and external stimuli. Motivation serves as a catalyst for engaging in emotion regulation strategies, such as cognitive reappraisal, problem-solving, and relaxation techniques, that help individuals cope with stress, regulate their moods, and maintain emotional balance. For example, individuals who are motivated to maintain a positive outlook on life may actively seek out opportunities for gratitude practice, positive visualization, or mindfulness meditation to cultivate a more optimistic mindset and regulate their emotions effectively. Their motivation to experience positive emotions and reduce negative ones drives their efforts to regulate their emotional experiences and responses.

Motivation serves as a catalyst for developing and enhancing emotional intelligence skills, driving individuals to engage in self-awareness, social awareness, self-management, and relationship management efforts that promote emotional well-being and interpersonal effectiveness. By recognizing the role of motivation in emotional intelligence and harnessing it effectively, individuals can cultivate greater self-awareness, empathy, resilience, and social competence, leading to greater success and fulfillment in both personal and professional domains. Motivation plays a crucial role in emotional intelligence by influencing individuals' ability to recognize, understand, and manage emotions in themselves and others. Whether driven by intrinsic or extrinsic factors, motivation serves as a driving force behind EI competencies, shaping individuals' attitudes, goals, and behaviors in ways that promote emotional well-being, interpersonal relationships, and personal growth. By recognizing the role of motivation in emotional intelligence and harnessing it effectively, individuals can develop and enhance their EI skills, leading to greater success and fulfillment in both personal and professional domains.

Enhancing Your Motivation

Enhancing motivation is essential for achieving personal and professional goals, overcoming obstacles, and maintaining a sense of fulfillment and purpose in life. Motivation serves as the driving force behind goal-directed behavior, influencing individuals' attitudes, efforts, and persistence in pursuing desired outcomes. Whether striving for academic success, career advancement, or personal growth, enhancing motivation can help individuals stay focused, energized, and committed to their aspirations. In this discussion, we'll explore various strategies and techniques for enhancing motivation effectively.

1. **Clarify Your Goals:** One of the first steps in enhancing motivation is clarifying your goals and identifying what you truly want to achieve. Clearly defined goals provide direction, focus, and purpose, helping you prioritize your efforts and allocate resources effectively. Take the time to reflect on your values, interests, and aspirations,

and set specific, measurable, achievable, relevant, and time-bound (SMART) goals that align with your vision for the future.

2. **Connect with Your Values:** Connecting with your values can enhance motivation by tapping into what truly matters to you on a deeper level. Reflect on the values that guide your decisions, actions, and priorities in life, and consider how your goals align with these values. When your goals are aligned with your values, you are more likely to feel a sense of intrinsic motivation, passion, and purpose in pursuing them.
3. **Find Your Why:** Understanding your "why" can provide a powerful source of motivation and inspiration. Take the time to explore the underlying reasons behind your goals and aspirations, and identify the deeper meaning or purpose driving your desire to achieve them. Knowing why your goals are important to you can fuel your motivation, increase your resilience, and help you stay focused and committed, even when faced with challenges or setbacks.
4. **Set Meaningful Rewards:** Setting meaningful rewards can enhance motivation by providing incentives and reinforcement for progress and achievement. Identify rewards that are personally meaningful and motivating to you, whether they involve tangible rewards such as treats or experiences, or intangible rewards such as feelings of pride or satisfaction. Use rewards to celebrate milestones, acknowledge progress, and maintain momentum toward your goals.
5. **Break It Down:** Breaking your goals down into smaller, more manageable tasks can enhance motivation by reducing overwhelm and increasing feelings of competence and progress. Create a

step-by-step action plan outlining the specific tasks and milestones required to achieve your goals, and focus on completing one task at a time. Celebrate small victories along the way to maintain motivation and momentum.

6. **Create a Supportive Environment:** Creating a supportive environment can enhance motivation by surrounding yourself with people, resources, and structures that foster success. Seek out social support from friends, family members, or mentors who encourage and believe in you. Create a workspace or routine that minimizes distractions and maximizes focus and productivity. Invest in tools, resources, or training that support your goals and help you overcome obstacles.

7. **Visualize Success:** Visualization techniques can enhance motivation by mentally rehearsing success and envisioning yourself achieving your goals. Take time each day to visualize yourself making progress, overcoming challenges, and ultimately achieving your desired outcomes. Imagine the emotions, sensations, and experiences associated with success, and use visualization to reinforce your motivation and confidence.

8. **Cultivate a Growth Mindset:** Cultivating a growth mindset can enhance motivation by reframing challenges as opportunities for learning and growth. Embrace the belief that your abilities and intelligence can be developed through effort, practice, and persistence, rather than being fixed or innate. Approach setbacks and failures as valuable learning experiences that can ultimately strengthen your resilience and motivation.

9. **Stay Flexible and Adapt:** Staying flexible and adaptable can enhance motivation by allowing you

to adjust your goals, strategies, and expectations in response to changing circumstances. Be willing to reassess your goals and priorities periodically, and adjust your plans accordingly based on new information or feedback. Embrace a mindset of continuous improvement and adaptation, and view challenges and setbacks as opportunities for growth and learning.

10. **Celebrate Progress:** Finally, celebrating progress along the way can enhance motivation by reinforcing positive behaviors and achievements. Take time to acknowledge and celebrate your successes, no matter how small, and use them as fuel to propel you forward. Recognize the effort, dedication, and resilience that you've demonstrated, and use each success as motivation to continue pursuing your goals with confidence and enthusiasm.

In conclusion, enhancing motivation is essential for achieving personal and professional goals, overcoming obstacles, and maintaining a sense of fulfillment and purpose in life. By clarifying your goals, connecting with your values, finding your why, setting meaningful rewards, breaking it down, creating a supportive environment, visualizing success, cultivating a growth mindset, staying flexible and adaptable, and celebrating progress, you can enhance your motivation and increase your chances of success in pursuing your aspirations.

Setting SMART Goals

Setting SMART goals is a powerful strategy for clarifying objectives, increasing motivation, and achieving success in various aspects of life. SMART is an acronym that stands for Specific, Measurable, Achievable, Relevant, and Time-bound, and these criteria help individuals create goals that are clear, actionable, and attainable. In this discussion, we'll explore each component of SMART goals and how they contribute to effective goal setting.

1. **Specific:** The "S" in SMART goals stands for specific, emphasizing the importance of clearly defining what you want to achieve. Specific goals are focused and well-defined, leaving no room for ambiguity or confusion. When setting specific goals, ask yourself the following questions:
    - What exactly do I want to accomplish?
    - Why is this goal important to me?
    - What are the key actions or outcomes involved?
    - Who else needs to be involved or informed?

For example, instead of setting a vague goal like "exercise more," a specific goal would be "exercise for 30 minutes three times a week."

2. **Measurable:** The "M" in SMART goals stands for measurable, highlighting the importance of establishing concrete criteria for assessing progress and success. Measurable goals are quantifiable and observable, allowing you to track your progress over time and determine whether you're on track to achieve your objectives. When setting measurable goals, consider the following:
    - How will I know when I've achieved my goal?
    - What specific metrics or indicators will I use to measure progress?
    - How frequently will I assess my progress toward the goal?
    - What benchmarks or milestones will I use to track my progress?

Using the previous example, you could measure progress by tracking the number of exercise sessions completed each week or monitoring improvements in fitness levels over time.

3. **Achievable:** The "A" in SMART goals stands for achievable, emphasizing the importance of setting goals that are realistic and attainable given your resources, abilities, and constraints. Achievable goals are challenging yet within reach, motivating you to stretch beyond your comfort zone without setting yourself up for failure. When assessing the achievability of your goals, consider the following:
    - Do I have the necessary skills, knowledge, and resources to achieve this goal?
    - Is this goal aligned with my current commitments, priorities, and constraints?
    - What potential obstacles or challenges might I encounter, and how can I address them?
    - What steps can I take to increase my likelihood of success?

It's essential to set goals that push you outside of your comfort zone but are still within the realm of possibility with effort and commitment.

4. **Relevant:** The "R" in SMART goals stands for relevant, emphasizing the importance of setting goals that are meaningful, aligned with your values, and relevant to your broader objectives. Relevant goals contribute to your overall vision, purpose, and aspirations, keeping you focused and motivated to pursue them. When assessing the relevance of your goals, consider the following:
    - Does this goal align with my values, interests, and long-term objectives?
    - How does this goal contribute to my personal or professional growth?

- Are there other goals or priorities that I should focus on instead?
- Will achieving this goal have a meaningful impact on my life or the lives of others?

Setting relevant goals ensures that you're investing your time and energy in pursuits that matter to you and align with your larger aspirations.

5. **Time-bound:** The "T" in SMART goals stands for time-bound, emphasizing the importance of setting deadlines or timeframes for achieving your objectives. Time-bound goals have a clear start and end point, creating a sense of urgency and accountability that helps you stay focused and motivated. When setting time-bound goals, consider the following:
    - When do I want to achieve this goal? What is my target completion date?
    - What specific milestones or checkpoints will I use to track my progress over time?
    - How will I break down the goal into smaller, actionable tasks and allocate time for each?
    - What potential obstacles or distractions might arise, and how can I manage my time effectively to stay on track?

Setting time-bound goals helps you prioritize your efforts, manage your time efficiently, and maintain momentum toward achieving your objectives.

Setting SMART goals is a powerful strategy for clarifying objectives, increasing motivation, and achieving success in various areas of life. By ensuring that your goals are specific, measurable, achievable, relevant, and time-bound, you can create a roadmap for success that keeps you focused, motivated, and accountable. Whether pursuing personal or professional aspirations, SMART goal setting can help you turn your dreams into reality and unlock your full potential.

Building Resilience and Perseverance

Building resilience and perseverance is essential for navigating life's challenges, overcoming obstacles, and achieving long-term success and fulfillment. Resilience refers to the ability to adapt and bounce back from adversity, while perseverance involves the persistence and determination to pursue goals despite setbacks or difficulties. By developing these qualities, individuals can cultivate greater mental and emotional strength, enhance their coping skills, and thrive in the face of adversity.

1. **Cultivate a Growth Mindset:** Cultivating a growth mindset is essential for building resilience and perseverance. Embrace the belief that challenges and failures are opportunities for learning and growth rather than indicators of fixed abilities or limitations. Adopt a positive attitude toward setbacks, view them as temporary setbacks rather than insurmountable obstacles, and focus on what you can learn and how you can improve from the experience.
2. **Develop Self-Awareness:** Developing self-awareness is crucial for building resilience and perseverance. Take time to reflect on your thoughts, emotions, and behaviors in response to adversity, and identify your strengths, weaknesses, and coping strategies. By understanding your reactions and patterns of behavior, you can better manage stress, regulate your emotions, and develop effective coping mechanisms for dealing with challenges.
3. **Build a Supportive Network:** Building a supportive network of friends, family members, mentors, and colleagues is essential for building

resilience and perseverance. Surround yourself with positive, encouraging individuals who believe in your abilities and offer support, guidance, and encouragement during difficult times. Lean on your support network for emotional support, practical advice, and perspective when facing challenges or setbacks.

4. **Practice Self-Care:** Practicing self-care is essential for building resilience and perseverance. Take care of your physical, mental, and emotional well-being by prioritizing activities that nourish and replenish your energy reserves. Get regular exercise, eat a balanced diet, get enough sleep, and engage in activities that bring you joy and relaxation. Make time for activities that recharge your batteries and help you cope with stress more effectively.

5. **Set Realistic Goals:** Setting realistic goals is crucial for building resilience and perseverance. Break down your goals into smaller, more manageable tasks, and set realistic timelines and expectations for achieving them. Focus on making progress one step at a time, and celebrate small victories along the way to maintain motivation and momentum. Adjust your goals and strategies as needed based on feedback, setbacks, and changing circumstances.

6. **Develop Problem-Solving Skills:** Developing problem-solving skills is essential for building resilience and perseverance. Approach challenges and setbacks as opportunities to problem-solve and find creative solutions rather than obstacles to be avoided or ignored. Break down complex problems into smaller, more manageable steps, and brainstorm potential solutions or alternatives. Seek input from others, gather information, and

weigh the pros and cons of different options before taking action.

7. **Practice Mindfulness and Stress Management:** Practicing mindfulness and stress management techniques is essential for building resilience and perseverance. Incorporate mindfulness practices such as deep breathing, meditation, or visualization into your daily routine to reduce stress, increase self-awareness, and promote emotional well-being. Learn to recognize and manage stress triggers, and develop healthy coping mechanisms for dealing with stress effectively.
8. **Learn from Failure and Setbacks:** Learning from failure and setbacks is essential for building resilience and perseverance. Embrace failure as a natural part of the learning process, and use setbacks as opportunities for growth and self-improvement. Analyze what went wrong, identify lessons learned, and adjust your approach or strategy accordingly. By viewing failure as feedback rather than defeat, you can bounce back stronger and more resilient than before.
9. **Maintain a Positive Outlook:** Maintaining a positive outlook is essential for building resilience and perseverance. Cultivate optimism and hopefulness, and focus on the opportunities and possibilities that arise from challenges and setbacks. Practice gratitude, optimism, and self-compassion, and remind yourself of your strengths, accomplishments, and past successes when facing adversity. By maintaining a positive attitude, you can cultivate resilience and persevere through even the toughest of times.

Building resilience and perseverance is essential for navigating life's challenges, overcoming obstacles, and achieving long-term success and fulfillment. By cultivating a growth mindset, developing self-awareness, building a supportive network, practicing self-care, setting realistic goals, developing problem-solving skills, practicing mindfulness and stress management, learning from failure and setbacks, and maintaining a positive outlook, individuals can cultivate greater mental and emotional strength, enhance their coping skills, and thrive in the face of adversity.

4

Empathy

What is Empathy?

Empathy is a fundamental aspect of human interaction and understanding, often described as the ability to perceive, understand, and share the feelings, thoughts, and perspectives of others. It involves both cognitive and emotional components, allowing individuals to not only recognize and comprehend others' emotions but also to respond to them with compassion and sensitivity.

At its core, empathy involves stepping into someone else's shoes and seeing the world through their eyes. It requires individuals to suspend their own judgments and biases, tune into others' experiences, and validate their feelings and experiences without passing judgment. Empathy involves actively listening to others, demonstrating understanding and support, and offering comfort and encouragement when needed.

Empathy is often distinguished from sympathy, which involves feeling compassion or pity for someone else's suffering without necessarily fully understanding or sharing their perspective. Unlike sympathy, which can sometimes be more passive or detached, empathy involves a deeper level of engagement and connection with others' emotions and experiences.

Empathy plays a crucial role in various aspects of human interaction and relationships, including:

1. **Building Relationships:** Empathy is essential for forming strong, meaningful connections with others. By demonstrating understanding, compassion, and support, individuals can foster trust, intimacy, and mutual respect in their relationships.
2. **Effective Communication:** Empathy enhances communication by helping individuals understand others' perspectives and respond to their needs and emotions appropriately. Empathetic listening involves not only hearing what others are saying but also tuning into their underlying feelings and emotions.
3. **Conflict Resolution:** Empathy is key to resolving conflicts and disagreements constructively. By empathizing with others' viewpoints and emotions, individuals can find common ground, validate each other's experiences, and work together to find mutually acceptable solutions.
4. **Leadership and Collaboration:** Empathy is an essential trait for effective leadership and collaboration. Leaders who demonstrate empathy are better able to understand and respond to the needs and concerns of their team members, foster a positive and inclusive work environment, and inspire trust and loyalty among their followers.

5. **Cultural Competence:** Empathy is crucial for promoting cultural competence and understanding in diverse societies. By empathizing with individuals from different cultural backgrounds, individuals can bridge cultural divides, reduce prejudice and discrimination, and promote mutual understanding and respect.

Overall, empathy is a fundamental aspect of human relationships and society, contributing to compassion, understanding, and connection among individuals. By cultivating empathy in their interactions with others, individuals can foster deeper relationships, enhance communication and collaboration, and contribute to a more compassionate and inclusive world.

Importance of Empathy in Emotional Intelligence

Empathy is widely recognized as a cornerstone of emotional intelligence (EI), playing a crucial role in various aspects of emotional competence and interpersonal relationships. The importance of empathy in emotional intelligence stems from its ability to facilitate understanding, connection, and effective communication with others. Here are several key reasons why empathy is essential in emotional intelligence:

1. **Understanding Others:** Empathy enables individuals to understand the emotions, perspectives, and experiences of others. By empathizing with others, individuals can put themselves in someone else's shoes, seeing the world from their point of view. This understanding fosters deeper connections and allows individuals to respond to others with compassion, sensitivity, and insight.

2. **Building Relationships:** Empathy is essential for building and maintaining healthy, fulfilling relationships. When individuals demonstrate

empathy, they show others that their feelings and experiences are valid and respected. This fosters trust, intimacy, and mutual respect, strengthening the bonds between individuals and promoting positive interactions and collaboration.

3. **Effective Communication:** Empathy enhances communication by helping individuals accurately interpret and respond to others' emotions and cues. Empathetic listening involves not only hearing what others are saying but also understanding the underlying feelings and needs behind their words. This enables individuals to communicate more effectively, express empathy and support, and navigate interpersonal interactions with sensitivity and understanding.

4. **Conflict Resolution:** Empathy plays a crucial role in resolving conflicts and disagreements constructively. When individuals empathize with others' perspectives and emotions, they can find common ground, validate each other's experiences, and work together to find mutually acceptable solutions. Empathy helps de-escalate conflicts, promote understanding, and foster compromise and reconciliation.

5. **Leadership and Influence:** Empathy is an essential trait for effective leadership and influence. Leaders who demonstrate empathy are better able to understand and respond to the needs and concerns of their team members, inspire trust and loyalty, and foster a positive and inclusive work environment. Empathetic leaders can motivate and empower others, build strong relationships, and drive positive change within organizations.

6. **Emotional Regulation:** Empathy contributes to emotional regulation by helping individuals

manage their own emotions and respond empathetically to others' emotional cues. When individuals empathize with others, they develop greater emotional awareness and regulation skills, enabling them to navigate interpersonal interactions more effectively and maintain positive relationships even in challenging situations.

In conclusion, empathy is a fundamental component of emotional intelligence, playing a crucial role in understanding others, building relationships, communicating effectively, resolving conflicts, and influencing others positively. By cultivating empathy, individuals can enhance their emotional intelligence skills, foster deeper connections with others, and thrive in both personal and professional domains.

Types of Empathy: Cognitive, Emotional, and Compassionate

Empathy is a complex psychological phenomenon that involves understanding and sharing the emotions, thoughts, and perspectives of others. While empathy is often discussed as a unified concept, researchers have identified different types or components of empathy that capture distinct aspects of this phenomenon. Three primary types of empathy are commonly recognized: cognitive empathy, emotional empathy, and compassionate empathy. Each type of empathy involves unique processes and responses, contributing to individuals' ability to connect with and understand others.

1. **Cognitive Empathy:** Cognitive empathy, also known as perspective-taking or mentalizing, refers to the ability to understand and intellectually grasp another person's emotions, thoughts, and perspective. It involves putting oneself in someone else's shoes and imagining what they might be thinking or feeling. Cognitive empathy relies on

higher-order cognitive processes, such as theory of mind and perspective-taking abilities, to accurately interpret and understand others' mental states.

Cognitive empathy, also known as perspective-taking or mentalizing, is a component of empathy that involves understanding and intellectually grasping another person's emotions, thoughts, and perspectives. It refers to the ability to put oneself in someone else's shoes and imagine what they might be thinking or feeling without necessarily sharing the same emotional experience. Cognitive empathy relies on higher-order cognitive processes, such as theory of mind and perspective-taking abilities, to accurately interpret and understand others' mental states.

Individuals with strong cognitive empathy skills are adept at recognizing and interpreting social cues, such as facial expressions, body language, and tone of voice, to infer others' emotions and intentions. They can imagine themselves in others' situations and anticipate their thoughts, feelings, and reactions based on contextual information and social cues.

Cognitive empathy plays a crucial role in social cognition, communication, and interpersonal relationships. It allows individuals to navigate social interactions effectively, understand others' perspectives, and respond empathetically to their needs and experiences. By accurately interpreting and understanding others' mental states, individuals with strong cognitive empathy skills can build rapport, foster trust, and establish meaningful connections with others.

In addition to its role in interpersonal relationships, cognitive empathy is also important for empathy-related abilities, such as moral reasoning, social decision-making, and conflict resolution. It enables individuals to consider others' perspectives, weigh different viewpoints, and make informed judgments about ethical and social issues.

Cognitive empathy should be distinguished from emotional empathy, which involves sharing and vicariously experiencing others' emotions, and compassionate empathy, which involves feeling genuine concern and taking action to alleviate others' suffering. While cognitive empathy focuses on understanding others' mental states from an intellectual standpoint, emotional and compassionate empathy involve more affective and motivational components.

Overall, cognitive empathy is a valuable skill that enhances individuals' ability to understand and connect with others in diverse social contexts. By developing and nurturing cognitive empathy skills, individuals can improve their social cognition, communication, and interpersonal relationships, ultimately fostering greater empathy, understanding, and compassion in their interactions with others.

Example: A person with strong cognitive empathy might be able to recognize that a friend is feeling anxious based on their facial expressions, body language, and verbal cues, even if they do not share the same emotional experience.

2. **Emotional Empathy:** Emotional empathy, also known as affective empathy or empathic concern, refers to the ability to share and vicariously experience the emotions of others. It involves feeling a similar emotional response to someone else's emotional state, often without consciously reasoning about or analyzing the situation. Emotional empathy relies on the activation of mirror neurons and emotional contagion processes, which allow individuals to resonate with and "feel with" others.

> Emotional empathy, also known as affective empathy or empathic concern, is a component of empathy that involves sharing and vicariously experiencing the emotions of others. It refers to the ability to resonate with and "feel with" someone else's emotional state, often without consciously reasoning about or analyzing the situation. Emotional empathy relies on the activation of mirror neurons and emotional contagion processes, which allow individuals to experience a similar emotional response to someone else's emotional experiences.

Individuals with strong emotional empathy skills are highly attuned to others' emotional states and can easily pick up on subtle emotional cues, such as facial expressions, vocal tone, and body language. They may find themselves automatically mirroring or "feeling" the emotions of those around them, even if they have not directly experienced the same situation.

Emotional empathy allows individuals to connect with others on a deep, emotional level and to share in their joys, sorrows, and struggles. It fosters a sense of compassion, understanding, and solidarity with others, as individuals recognize and validate the emotional experiences of those around them.

While emotional empathy can be a powerful force for connection and compassion, it can also have drawbacks if individuals become overwhelmed or excessively absorbed in others' emotions. Empathizing too strongly with others' negative emotions may lead to emotional distress or burnout, particularly in caregiving professions or situations involving high levels of emotional intensity.

Emotional empathy should be distinguished from cognitive empathy, which involves understanding and intellectually grasping others' emotions and perspectives, and compassionate empathy, which involves feeling genuine concern and taking action to alleviate others' suffering. While cognitive empathy focuses on understanding others' mental states from a cognitive standpoint, emotional empathy involves a more affective or emotional response to others' emotions.

Overall, emotional empathy is a valuable skill that enhances individuals' ability to connect with and understand others on an emotional level. By developing and nurturing emotional empathy skills, individuals can foster greater compassion, empathy, and connection in their interpersonal relationships, ultimately contributing to a more empathetic and supportive social environment.

Example: A person with strong emotional empathy might feel sad or tearful when witnessing a friend's grief or distress, even if they have not directly experienced the same situation.

3. **Compassionate Empathy:** Compassionate empathy, sometimes referred to as empathic or altruistic action, goes beyond understanding and sharing others' emotions to include a desire to alleviate their suffering or distress. It involves feeling genuine concern and empathy for others' well-being and taking action to support or help them in meaningful ways. Compassionate empathy combines elements of both cognitive and emotional empathy with prosocial behavior and altruistic motivation.

   Compassionate empathy, also known as empathic or altruistic action, combines elements of both cognitive and emotional empathy with prosocial behavior and altruistic motivation. It goes beyond understanding and sharing others' emotions to include a genuine desire to alleviate their suffering or distress. Compassionate empathy involves feeling empathy and concern for others' well-being and taking action to support or help them in meaningful ways.

Individuals with strong compassionate empathy skills not only recognize and understand others' emotions and experiences but also feel a deep sense of compassion and empathy for those who are suffering or in need. They are motivated by a genuine desire to alleviate others' suffering and make a positive difference in their lives, often going out of their way to offer support, comfort, or assistance.

Compassionate empathy involves both affective and behavioral components, including:

1. **Affective Component:** The affective component of compassionate empathy refers to the emotional response of feeling concern, compassion, or empathy for others' suffering or distress. It involves resonating with others' emotions and experiencing a genuine sense of caring and empathy for their well-being.
2. **Behavioral Component:** The behavioral component of compassionate empathy involves taking action to support or help others in meaningful ways. This may include offering emotional support, providing practical assistance, or engaging in acts of kindness or generosity to alleviate others' suffering and improve their situation.

Compassionate empathy is a key driver of prosocial behavior and altruistic acts of kindness, generosity, and compassion. It motivates individuals to reach out to others in need, offer support and assistance, and make a positive difference in their lives. Compassionate empathy is closely linked to moral values such as kindness, compassion, and altruism, and it plays a crucial role in fostering empathy, compassion, and cooperation in interpersonal relationships and social interactions.

While compassionate empathy is a powerful force for good, it's important for individuals to maintain boundaries and self-care to prevent burnout or emotional exhaustion. Engaging in compassionate acts of empathy and altruism can be emotionally taxing, particularly in situations involving high levels of suffering or distress. Practicing self-compassion, setting boundaries, and seeking support from others can help individuals maintain their well-being while still engaging in compassionate acts of empathy and kindness.

Overall, compassionate empathy is a valuable skill that enhances individuals' ability to connect with and support others in meaningful ways. By cultivating compassionate empathy skills, individuals can foster greater empathy, compassion, and kindness in their interpersonal relationships, ultimately contributing to a more caring and supportive social environment.

Example: A person with compassionate empathy might offer comfort, support, or assistance to a friend who is struggling, demonstrating a genuine desire to alleviate their suffering and improve their situation.

It is important to note that while cognitive, emotional, and compassionate empathy are distinct types, they are often interconnected and can influence one another in complex ways. Individuals may vary in their levels of each type of empathy, with some people naturally exhibiting stronger cognitive empathy, emotional empathy, or compassionate empathy based on their personality traits, upbringing, and life experiences. Developing and nurturing all three types of empathy can enhance individuals' ability to connect with and understand others, fostering deeper relationships, empathy, and compassion in interpersonal interactions.

The Role of Empathy in Relationships

Empathy plays a foundational role in relationships, serving as a cornerstone for understanding, connection, and intimacy between individuals. It involves the ability to perceive, understand, and share the emotions, thoughts, and perspectives of others, fostering a deeper sense of understanding and compassion in interpersonal interactions.

1. **Fostering Understanding and Connection:** Empathy is essential for fostering understanding and connection in relationships. By empathizing with each other's emotions and experiences, individuals can develop a deeper appreciation for their partner's perspective and feelings. Empathetic listening involves actively tuning into and validating each other's emotions, demonstrating care, respect, and support in the process. This fosters a sense of emotional intimacy and mutual understanding, strengthening the bond between partners and deepening their connection.

2. **Enhancing Communication:** Empathy is a vital component of effective communication in relationships. When individuals demonstrate empathy, they not only listen attentively to their partner's words but also seek to understand the underlying emotions and meanings behind them. Empathetic communication involves validating and acknowledging each other's feelings, expressing understanding and support, and responding with empathy and sensitivity. This promotes open, honest, and authentic communication, allowing partners to express themselves freely and feel heard and understood in the process.

3. **Promoting Conflict Resolution:** Empathy is

crucial for resolving conflicts and disagreements constructively in relationships. When conflicts arise, empathetic partners are better able to understand and empathize with each other's perspectives and emotions, even when they disagree. Empathetic listening helps partners communicate their needs, concerns, and feelings more effectively, reducing defensiveness and promoting empathy and understanding. By empathizing with each other's experiences and finding common ground, partners can work together to find mutually acceptable solutions and strengthen their relationship in the process.

4. **Cultivating Intimacy and Trust:** Empathy is a key driver of intimacy and trust in relationships. When partners demonstrate empathy toward each other, they create a safe and supportive emotional environment where they can be vulnerable and authentic with each other. Empathetic validation of each other's emotions and experiences fosters a sense of trust and security, reassuring partners that they are accepted and valued for who they are. This deepens the emotional bond between partners, fostering a sense of closeness, intimacy, and connection that enhances relationship satisfaction and longevity.

5. **Nurturing Emotional Support:** Empathy is instrumental in providing emotional support and validation to partners in times of need. When one partner is experiencing distress or difficulty, empathetic listening and support from the other partner can provide comfort, reassurance, and validation of their feelings. Empathy involves being present for each other emotionally, offering empathy, understanding, and encouragement, and providing a safe space for partners to express themselves authentically. This fosters a sense of

emotional closeness and support, strengthening the emotional connection between partners and promoting resilience in the face of challenges.

6. **Building Empathy Skills:** Cultivating empathy skills is essential for maintaining healthy, fulfilling relationships. Empathy is not only a natural inclination but also a skill that can be developed and honed through practice and intention. Partners can enhance their empathy skills by actively listening to each other, practicing perspective-taking, and validating each other's emotions and experiences. Engaging in empathy-building exercises, such as role-playing or reflective listening, can also help partners develop greater empathy and understanding for each other.
7. **Respecting Differences and Individuality:** Empathy encourages partners to respect and honor each other's differences, perspectives, and individuality. By empathizing with each other's unique experiences and viewpoints, partners can celebrate their differences and appreciate each other's strengths and weaknesses. Empathy promotes acceptance, tolerance, and respect in relationships, allowing partners to embrace each other's differences and grow together as individuals and as a couple.

Empathy plays a multifaceted role in relationships, serving as a foundation for understanding, connection, and intimacy between partners. By fostering understanding and connection, enhancing communication, promoting conflict resolution, cultivating intimacy and trust, providing emotional support, building empathy skills, and respecting differences and individuality, empathy contributes to healthy, fulfilling relationships characterized by mutual respect, understanding, and support. Partners who demonstrate empathy toward each other create a strong emotional bond, navigate challenges effectively, and experience greater satisfaction and fulfillment in their relationship.

Developing Empathy

Developing empathy is an ongoing process that involves cultivating awareness, understanding, and compassion for others' emotions, thoughts, and experiences. While some individuals may naturally possess strong empathetic abilities, empathy is a skill that can be developed and enhanced through practice, self-reflection, and intentional effort.

1. **Practice Active Listening:** Active listening is a foundational skill for developing empathy. It involves fully engaging with others when they speak, focusing on their words, tone, and body language, and demonstrating genuine interest and attention. Practice active listening by maintaining eye contact, nodding in acknowledgment, and paraphrasing or summarizing what others have said to ensure understanding. Avoid interrupting or jumping to conclusions, and give others the space to express themselves fully without judgment or criticism.

2. **Cultivate Curiosity and Open-Mindedness:** Cultivating curiosity and open-mindedness is essential for developing empathy. Approach interactions with others with a sense of genuine curiosity and interest in their experiences, perspectives, and emotions. Ask open-ended questions to encourage others to share more about themselves and their thoughts and feelings. Be open to learning from others' perspectives, even if they differ from your own, and suspend judgment or preconceived notions to truly understand where they're coming from.

3. **Practice Perspective-Taking:** Perspective-taking is a key component of empathy that involves imagining oneself in someone else's shoes and seeing the world from their point of view. Practice perspective-taking by actively trying to understand others' thoughts, emotions, and experiences, even if they differ from your own. Consider how factors such as background, culture, and personal history may influence others' perspectives and reactions, and strive to empathize with their unique viewpoint.
4. **Develop Emotional Awareness:** Developing emotional awareness is crucial for empathy, as it allows individuals to recognize and understand their own emotions and those of others more effectively. Practice tuning into your own emotions and bodily sensations, and explore how they influence your thoughts and behaviors. Pay attention to others' verbal and nonverbal cues, such as facial expressions, gestures, and tone of voice, to discern their emotional states and respond with empathy and sensitivity.
5. **Engage in Perspective-Broadening Activities:** Engaging in perspective-broadening activities can help expand your empathy and understanding of diverse experiences and perspectives. Seek out opportunities to interact with individuals from different backgrounds, cultures, and life experiences, and actively listen to their stories and perspectives. Read books, watch films, or attend cultural events that expose you to different viewpoints and ways of life. Participate in diversity and inclusion training or workshops to learn more about systemic inequalities and social justice issues.
6. **Practice Empathetic Communication:**

Empathetic communication involves expressing understanding, validation, and support for others' emotions and experiences. Practice using empathetic language and gestures, such as acknowledging others' feelings, expressing empathy and concern, and offering support or encouragement. Use "I" statements to communicate your own emotions and experiences authentically, and avoid making assumptions or judgments about others' feelings or motivations.

7. **Cultivate Self-Compassion:** Cultivating self-compassion is essential for developing empathy, as it allows individuals to extend kindness, understanding, and compassion to themselves and others. Practice self-compassion by treating yourself with kindness and understanding when facing challenges or setbacks. Acknowledge your own emotions and experiences without judgment or self-criticism, and recognize that everyone experiences pain and suffering at times. By cultivating self-compassion, you can develop greater empathy and compassion for others as well.

In conclusion, developing empathy is a lifelong journey that involves cultivating awareness, understanding, and compassion for others' emotions, thoughts, and experiences. By practicing active listening, cultivating curiosity and open-mindedness, practicing perspective-taking, developing emotional awareness, engaging in perspective-broadening activities, practicing empathetic communication, and cultivating self-compassion, individuals can enhance their empathy skills and foster deeper connections and understanding in their interpersonal relationships.

Active Listening Skills

Active listening skills refer to a set of techniques and

behaviors used to fully engage with and understand what someone else is saying. It's a communication skill that involves not only hearing the words spoken but also paying attention to the speaker's tone, body language, and underlying emotions. Active listening requires concentration, empathy, and a genuine desire to understand the speaker's message. By actively listening, individuals can build rapport, strengthen relationships, and communicate more effectively with others.

Active listening is a fundamental communication skill that involves fully engaging with and understanding what others are saying. It is more than just hearing words; it's about giving full attention to the speaker, understanding their message, and demonstrating empathy and understanding. Here are some key active listening skills and techniques:

1. **Pay Attention:** Give the speaker your full attention by maintaining eye contact, facing them directly, and eliminating distractions such as phones or other devices. Show that you're interested and engaged in what they're saying through your body language and facial expressions.

2. **Listen Without Interrupting:** Avoid interrupting or jumping in with your own thoughts or opinions while the speaker is talking. Let them finish their thoughts before responding, and resist the urge to interject with your own experiences or perspectives.

3. **Paraphrase and Summarize:** Use paraphrasing and summarizing techniques to demonstrate that you're actively listening and understanding the speaker's message. Repeat back what they've said in your own words to confirm understanding and show that you're following along.

4. **Reflect Feelings:** Reflect the speaker's feelings and emotions back to them to show empathy and understanding. Acknowledge and validate their emotions by saying things like, "It sounds like you're feeling frustrated," or "I can see why that would make you feel proud."

5. **Ask Open-Ended Questions:** Encourage the speaker to elaborate and share more by asking open-ended questions that can't be answered with a simple yes or no. This shows that you're interested in hearing more about their thoughts and experiences and encourages deeper conversation.

6. **Use Nonverbal Cues:** Pay attention to nonverbal cues such as body language, facial expressions, and tone of voice to pick up on underlying emotions and messages. Show empathy and understanding through your own nonverbal cues, such as nodding or leaning in attentively.

7. **Provide Feedback:** Offer feedback and validation to the speaker to show that you're actively listening and understanding their message. Reflect back what you've heard, ask clarifying questions if needed, and offer support or encouragement as appropriate.

8. **Stay Neutral and Non-Judgmental:** Maintain a neutral and non-judgmental attitude while listening, even if you disagree with the speaker's opinions or perspectives. Listen with an open mind and avoid making assumptions or jumping to conclusions.

9. **Practice Empathy:** Put yourself in the speaker's shoes and try to understand their thoughts, feelings, and experiences from their perspective. Show empathy and compassion by acknowledging their emotions and validating their experiences.

10. **Be Patient and Respectful:** Be patient and respectful while listening, even if the conversation is challenging or difficult. Allow the speaker to express themselves fully and take the time they need to communicate their message.

By honing these active listening skills and techniques, you can become a more effective and empathetic listener, fostering deeper connections, and understanding in your interpersonal relationships.

Perspective-Taking Exercises

Perspective-taking exercises are valuable tools for expanding our understanding and empathy towards others. These exercises involve stepping into someone else's shoes to see the world from their viewpoint. By doing so, we gain insight into their thoughts, emotions, and experiences, fostering empathy, compassion, and understanding.

Through role-playing scenarios, storytelling, empathy mapping, and other activities, perspective-taking exercises encourage us to consider different perspectives and challenge our own assumptions and biases. They help break down barriers, promote empathy, and strengthen relationships by fostering open-mindedness and mutual respect.

Engaging in perspective-taking exercises not only enhances our interpersonal skills but also promotes a more inclusive and empathetic society. By actively seeking to understand others' perspectives, we cultivate empathy and compassion, ultimately building stronger connections and fostering a culture of empathy and understanding.

Perspective-taking exercises are activities designed to help individuals develop empathy and understand others' perspectives more effectively. These exercises encourage individuals to imagine themselves in someone else's shoes and consider the world from their point of view. Here are some perspective-taking exercises:

1. **Role-Playing Scenarios:** Create role-playing scenarios where individuals take on different roles and perspectives. For example, participants could role-play a customer service interaction, with one person playing the customer and the other playing the service representative. This exercise helps participants see situations from different viewpoints and understand the challenges others may face.
2. **Storytelling and Sharing Experiences:** Encourage individuals to share personal stories and experiences from their own lives. This could be done through group discussions, storytelling circles, or writing exercises. Listening to others' stories helps individuals gain insight into different perspectives and experiences, fostering empathy and understanding.
3. **Empathy Mapping:** Use empathy mapping exercises to help individuals visualize and understand others' thoughts, feelings, and motivations. Participants create visual representations of someone else's perspective, including their needs, desires, fears, and challenges. This exercise helps individuals develop empathy by considering the factors that influence others' behavior and emotions.
4. **Writing from Different Perspectives:** Ask individuals to write from different perspectives, such as writing a letter or journal entry from the point of view of someone else. This exercise encourages individuals to imagine themselves in someone else's situation and consider how they might think and feel. It helps develop empathy and understanding for others' experiences.

5. **Cultural Immersion Activities:** Engage in cultural immersion activities that expose individuals to different cultures, lifestyles, and viewpoints. This could involve participating in cultural events, trying new foods, or learning about different traditions and customs. Immersing oneself in unfamiliar cultural contexts helps broaden perspectives and promote understanding of diverse viewpoints.
6. **Perspective-Taking Games:** Play perspective-taking games or activities that challenge individuals to see situations from different angles. For example, puzzle-solving games or team-building exercises where participants must work together to solve a problem from multiple perspectives. These games encourage collaboration, communication, and empathy.
7. **Reflective Journaling:** Encourage individuals to keep a reflective journal where they can write about their experiences, thoughts, and feelings. Journaling allows individuals to explore their own perspectives and biases while also considering alternative viewpoints. It promotes self-awareness and empathy by encouraging individuals to reflect on their own experiences and understand how they might differ from others'.

By engaging in perspective-taking exercises, individuals can develop empathy, understanding, and appreciation for others' perspectives. These exercises promote empathy, compassion, and communication skills, fostering stronger relationships and promoting a more inclusive and empathetic society.

Building Empathic Communication

Building empathic communication involves developing the skills and mindset necessary to create meaningful connections with others through understanding, validation, and empathy. It begins with actively listening to others, tuning into their emotions and experiences, and responding in a way that demonstrates empathy and understanding. Empathic communication fosters trust, respect, and mutual support in relationships, leading to deeper connections and greater emotional intimacy. By practicing empathy in our interactions with others, we create a more compassionate and inclusive environment where individuals feel heard, valued, and respected.

Building empathic communication involves fostering an environment where individuals feel heard, understood, and valued. It is about actively listening to others, expressing empathy and understanding, and communicating in a way that promotes trust, respect, and connection. Here are some strategies for building empathic communication:

1. **Practice Active Listening:** Focus on listening attentively to what the other person is saying, without interrupting or jumping to conclusions. Show genuine interest and engagement through your body language and verbal cues, such as nodding, maintaining eye contact, and asking clarifying questions.
2. **Validate Emotions:** Acknowledge and validate the other person's emotions and experiences, even if you don't agree with them. Reflect back what you've heard and express empathy and understanding for their feelings. For example, you might say, "It sounds like you're feeling frustrated. I can understand why that would be upsetting."
3. **Use Empathetic Language:** Choose your words carefully to convey empathy and understanding. Use phrases like "I understand," "I hear you," and "That must be difficult" to show that you're actively

listening and validating the other person's experiences.

4. **Avoid Judgment and Criticism:** Create a non-judgmental and supportive environment where individuals feel safe expressing themselves openly and honestly. Avoid criticizing or blaming others for their thoughts, feelings, or experiences, and instead focus on understanding and empathizing with their perspective.
5. **Practice Reflective Listening:** Use reflective listening techniques to demonstrate that you've understood the other person's message accurately. Paraphrase or summarize what they've said in your own words and ask for confirmation to ensure that you're on the same page.
6. **Show Empathy Through Body Language:** Pay attention to your body language and nonverbal cues to convey empathy and understanding. Use open and inviting gestures, such as nodding, leaning in, and maintaining an open posture, to show that you're engaged and attentive.
7. **Be Patient and Supportive:** Give the other person the time and space they need to express themselves fully, without rushing or pressuring them to communicate. Offer support and encouragement as needed, and let them know that you're there to listen and help in any way you can.
8. **Practice Self-Reflection:** Reflect on your own communication style and how it impacts your interactions with others. Be mindful of any biases or assumptions you may have and strive to approach conversations with an open mind and a willingness to learn from others' perspectives.
9. **Cultivate Empathy:** Develop your empathy skills

by putting yourself in others' shoes and considering their thoughts, feelings, and experiences from their perspective. Practice empathy in your daily interactions and seek opportunities to understand and connect with people from diverse backgrounds and viewpoints.

10. **Seek Feedback:** Ask for feedback from others about your communication style and how you can improve your empathic communication skills. Be open to constructive criticism and use it as an opportunity for growth and learning.

By incorporating these strategies into your communication style, you can build more empathic and compassionate relationships, fostering trust, understanding, and connection with others. Empathic communication promotes mutual respect, validation, and support, creating a positive and supportive environment where individuals feel valued and understood.

5

Social Skills

Understanding Social Skills

Understanding social skills is essential for navigating the complex web of human interactions and building meaningful relationships in various personal, academic, and professional settings. Social skills encompass a wide range of abilities and behaviors that enable individuals to effectively communicate, collaborate, empathize, and connect with others. In this comprehensive discussion, we'll explore the importance of social skills, the key components of social competence, and strategies for enhancing and applying these skills in different contexts.

Understanding social skills is essential for navigating the complexities of human interactions and fostering meaningful connections with others. Social skills encompass a wide range of abilities and behaviors that enable individuals to communicate effectively, build rapport, and navigate social situations with confidence and ease.

Key components of social skills include effective communication, empathy, assertiveness, and emotional intelligence. Strong communication skills involve both verbal and nonverbal cues, active listening, and the ability to express oneself clearly and confidently. Empathy allows individuals to understand and share others' emotions and perspectives, fostering deeper connections and mutual understanding. Assertiveness enables individuals to advocate for themselves, set boundaries, and assert their needs and opinions respectfully. Emotional intelligence involves recognizing and managing one's own emotions and those of others, contributing to positive interpersonal interactions and conflict resolution.

Developing social skills requires practice, self-awareness, and a willingness to learn and grow. By honing these skills, individuals can build stronger relationships, succeed academically and professionally, and navigate social situations with grace and confidence. Ultimately, understanding social skills empowers individuals to connect authentically, communicate effectively, and thrive in diverse social environments.

Definition of Social Skills

Social skills refer to a set of interpersonal abilities and behaviors that enable individuals to effectively navigate social interactions, communicate with others, and build and maintain relationships. These skills encompass a wide range of capabilities, including verbal and nonverbal communication, empathy, active listening, assertiveness, conflict resolution, and emotional intelligence.

Social skills are essential for successful interpersonal relationships in various contexts, such as personal, academic, and professional settings. They allow individuals to express themselves clearly, understand and respond to others' emotions and perspectives, and navigate social situations with confidence and ease. Strong social skills enable individuals to establish rapport, build trust, and collaborate effectively with others, leading to positive outcomes and fulfilling connections.

Developing social skills requires practice, self-awareness, and a willingness to learn and adapt. By honing these skills, individuals can enhance their communication abilities, cultivate empathy and understanding, and navigate the complexities of human relationships with confidence and grace. Ultimately, social skills play a critical role in fostering healthy and meaningful connections with others, contributing to personal well-being and overall success in life.

Importance of Social Skills

The importance of social skills cannot be overstated, as they are fundamental to navigating the complexities of human interactions and building meaningful relationships across various personal, academic, and professional domains. Social skills encompass a wide range of abilities and behaviors that enable individuals to communicate effectively, empathize with others, collaborate productively, and adapt to different social situations. Here's why social skills are crucial:

1. **Effective Communication:** Social skills are essential for effective communication, encompassing both verbal and nonverbal cues. Strong communication skills enable individuals to express themselves clearly, listen attentively, and convey their thoughts and feelings with confidence, fostering understanding and connection with others.
2. **Building Relationships:** Social skills play a

pivotal role in building and maintaining positive relationships with family, friends, colleagues, and acquaintances. They enable individuals to establish rapport, build trust, and connect with others on a deeper level, fostering intimacy, support, and mutual respect within interpersonal connections.

3. **Conflict Resolution:** Social skills are crucial for resolving conflicts and disagreements constructively. They enable individuals to navigate disagreements with empathy, assertiveness, and problem-solving skills, leading to peaceful resolution and strengthened relationships rather than escalation and discord.
4. **Emotional Intelligence:** Social skills are closely intertwined with emotional intelligence, which involves understanding and managing one's own emotions and those of others. High emotional intelligence enables individuals to navigate social situations with empathy, self-awareness, and resilience, fostering positive interactions and relationship dynamics.
5. **Academic Success:** Social skills are integral to academic success, as they facilitate collaboration, teamwork, and communication with peers, teachers, and classmates. Students with strong social skills are better equipped to participate in group projects, engage in class discussions, and form study groups, leading to improved learning outcomes and academic achievements.
6. **Career Advancement:** Social skills are highly valued in the workplace, as they contribute to professional success and advancement. Employees who possess strong social skills are better able to communicate persuasively, collaborate effectively, and interact positively with

colleagues, clients, and stakeholders, enhancing their prospects for career growth and leadership roles.

7. **Personal Well-Being:** Social skills contribute to overall personal well-being and quality of life. Individuals with strong social skills tend to experience greater satisfaction in their relationships, higher self-esteem, and a greater sense of belonging and connection within their communities, leading to enhanced mental and emotional well-being.

8. **Adaptability and Resilience:** Social skills enable individuals to adapt to different social situations and navigate changes and challenges with resilience. They empower individuals to interact confidently in diverse environments, build support networks, and overcome social obstacles and barriers, enhancing their ability to thrive in an ever-changing world.

In summary, social skills are indispensable for effective communication, relationship building, conflict resolution, emotional intelligence, academic success, career advancement, personal well-being, adaptability, and resilience. By developing and honing these skills, individuals can cultivate richer, more fulfilling lives characterized by strong connections, meaningful interactions, and positive contributions to society.

Components of Social Skills

The components of social skills encompass a broad range of abilities and behaviors that enable individuals to effectively navigate social interactions, communicate with others, and build and maintain relationships. While specific components may vary depending on context and cultural norms, some common elements of social skills include:

1. **Verbal Communication:** Verbal communication skills involve the ability to express oneself clearly and effectively using language. This includes speaking fluently, articulating thoughts and ideas coherently, and using appropriate vocabulary and grammar. Verbal communication also encompasses skills such as active listening, asking questions, and engaging in meaningful conversation.
2. **Nonverbal Communication:** Nonverbal communication plays a crucial role in social interactions and includes facial expressions, body language, gestures, and tone of voice. Nonverbal cues convey additional layers of meaning and can impact how messages are perceived and understood by others. Strong nonverbal communication skills involve being aware of and using body language effectively to enhance communication and express emotions.
3. **Empathy:** Empathy involves the ability to understand and share others' emotions and perspectives. It enables individuals to connect with others emotionally, show compassion, and respond sensitively to their needs and experiences. Empathy fosters understanding, connection, and mutual support in relationships, contributing to positive interactions and enhanced social well-being.
4. **Assertiveness:** Assertiveness is the ability to express one's thoughts, feelings, and needs confidently and respectfully, without being passive or aggressive. It involves advocating for oneself, setting boundaries, and standing up for what is important. Assertive communication promotes mutual respect, honesty, and assertiveness, leading to healthier and more balanced relationships.

5. **Active Listening:** Active listening is a fundamental social skill that involves fully engaging with and understanding what others are saying. It requires focused attention, empathy, and reflection, as well as the ability to paraphrase, summarize, and ask clarifying questions to demonstrate understanding. Active listening fosters deeper connections, trust, and effective communication in relationships.

6. **Problem-Solving:** Problem-solving skills are essential for resolving conflicts and disagreements in social interactions. They involve identifying and understanding the underlying issues, generating possible solutions, evaluating alternatives, and implementing strategies to address challenges constructively. Strong problem-solving skills enable individuals to navigate conflicts and disagreements with empathy, creativity, and flexibility, leading to positive outcomes and strengthened relationships.

7. **Adaptability:** Adaptability is the ability to adjust and respond effectively to changes and challenges in social situations. It involves being flexible, open-minded, and willing to consider different perspectives and approaches. Adaptability enables individuals to navigate diverse social environments, build rapport with others, and overcome obstacles and barriers with resilience and grace.

8. **Emotional Regulation:** Emotional regulation involves the ability to manage and express emotions appropriately in social interactions. It entails recognizing and understanding one's own emotions, as well as those of others, and responding in a manner that is calm, constructive, and respectful. Effective emotional regulation

promotes empathy, self-awareness, and emotional intelligence, enhancing social interactions and relationship dynamics.

These components of social skills collectively contribute to effective communication, relationship building, conflict resolution, and emotional intelligence, enabling individuals to navigate social interactions with confidence, empathy, and authenticity. By developing and honing these skills, individuals can cultivate richer, more fulfilling relationships and thrive in diverse social environments.

Strategies for Enhancing Social Skills

Enhancing social skills is essential for building strong relationships, succeeding in various aspects of life, and navigating social situations with confidence and ease. Here's a short note on strategies for enhancing social skills:

Improving social skills involves practice, self-awareness, and a willingness to learn and grow. Key strategies include active listening, empathy development, improving communication skills, building self-confidence, seeking feedback and support, practicing social skills in real-life situations, reflecting on experiences, role-playing and rehearsal, joining social skills groups or workshops, and using technology to practice. By incorporating these strategies into daily life, individuals can cultivate richer, more fulfilling relationships and thrive in diverse social environments.

Enhancing social skills involves deliberate practice, self-awareness, and a commitment to continuous improvement. Here are some strategies for enhancing social skills:

1. **Practice Active Listening:** Actively listen to others by giving them your full attention, maintaining eye contact, and avoiding

distractions. Practice empathetic listening, where you focus on understanding the speaker's emotions and perspectives. Ask clarifying questions and provide feedback to demonstrate that you are engaged and interested in what they have to say.

2. **Develop Empathy:** Cultivate empathy by putting yourself in others' shoes and imagining how they might be feeling. Pay attention to their verbal and nonverbal cues, validate their emotions, and respond with compassion and understanding. Practice perspective-taking to gain insight into different viewpoints and experiences.
3. **Improve Communication Skills:** Work on improving your verbal and nonverbal communication skills. Practice speaking clearly and confidently, using assertive language, and conveying your message effectively. Pay attention to your body language, facial expressions, and tone of voice to ensure that your nonverbal cues align with your verbal message.
4. **Build Self-Confidence:** Boost your self-confidence by setting realistic goals, challenging negative self-talk, and celebrating your successes. Practice assertiveness and self-expression in low-pressure situations, and gradually build your confidence in more challenging social scenarios.
5. **Seek Feedback and Support:** Solicit feedback from trusted friends, family members, or mentors about your social skills and areas for improvement. Consider seeking guidance from a counselor, coach, or social skills group to develop strategies for enhancing your social competence.
6. **Practice Social Skills in Real-Life Situations:** Put your social skills into practice in real-life situations by engaging in social activities, joining

clubs or organizations, and volunteering in your community. Take advantage of opportunities to interact with diverse groups of people and learn from their perspectives and experiences.

7. **Reflect and Learn from Experiences:** Reflect on your social interactions and experiences to identify patterns, strengths, and areas for growth. Learn from both successes and setbacks, and use them as opportunities for self-reflection and personal development. Keep a journal to track your progress and insights.
8. **Role-Playing and Rehearsal:** Practice social skills through role-playing exercises where you simulate different social scenarios and practice appropriate responses. Rehearse conversations and interactions in advance, especially if you anticipate challenging situations. This can help build confidence and reduce anxiety in real-life social encounters.
9. **Join Social Skills Groups or Workshops:** Consider participating in social skills groups or workshops where you can learn and practice social skills in a supportive environment. These groups often provide structured activities, feedback, and opportunities for skill-building exercises with peers facing similar challenges.
10. **Use Technology to Practice:** Take advantage of technology to practice social skills in virtual environments. Participate in online forums, social media groups, or video chat platforms to engage with others and practice communication and interaction skills in a low-pressure setting.

By incorporating these strategies into your daily life, you can enhance your social skills, build confidence in social situations, and cultivate deeper, more meaningful connections with others. Remember that improving social skills is a gradual process that requires patience, persistence, and a willingness to step outside your comfort zone.

Effective Communication Techniques

Effective communication techniques refer to strategies and methods used to convey messages clearly, accurately, and persuasively in various interpersonal, professional, and social interactions. These techniques are designed to facilitate understanding, foster meaningful connections, and achieve desired outcomes in communication. Effective communication techniques encompass a range of skills, including active listening, clarity and conciseness in speech or writing, empathy, assertiveness, nonverbal communication, adaptability, and conflict resolution. By employing these techniques, individuals can enhance their communication effectiveness, build rapport with others, and navigate social situations with confidence and proficiency.

Effective communication is essential for building strong relationships, fostering understanding, and achieving common goals. Here are some key techniques for effective communication:

1. **Active Listening:** Pay close attention to what the other person is saying without interrupting. Show interest through verbal and nonverbal cues, such as nodding and maintaining eye contact. Paraphrase or summarize their message to demonstrate understanding.
2. **Clarity and Conciseness:** Communicate your message clearly and succinctly, using simple and straightforward language. Avoid jargon or complex terminology that may confuse the listener. Organize your thoughts logically and present information in a structured manner.

3. **Empathy:** Put yourself in the other person's shoes and consider their perspective and feelings. Validate their emotions and demonstrate understanding and empathy. Use phrases such as "I understand how you feel" or "That must be difficult for you."
4. **Assertiveness:** Express your thoughts, feelings, and needs confidently and respectfully. Use "I" statements to communicate assertively without blaming or criticizing others. Set clear boundaries and stand up for yourself while considering the needs and feelings of others.
5. **Nonverbal Communication:** Pay attention to your body language, facial expressions, and tone of voice, as these can convey as much or more information than words. Maintain open and positive body language, such as facing the person you're speaking to and smiling.
6. **Active Engagement:** Encourage dialogue and participation by asking open-ended questions, seeking clarification, and inviting feedback. Show genuine interest in the other person's perspective and engage in two-way communication rather than monologuing.
7. **Respect and Courtesy:** Treat others with respect and courtesy, regardless of differences in opinion or background. Use polite language, listen without judgment, and avoid interrupting or speaking over others. Show appreciation for their contributions and perspectives.
8. **Feedback and Confirmation:** Provide feedback and confirmation to ensure mutual understanding. Repeat key points, ask for clarification if needed, and summarize the discussion to confirm agreement and alignment.

9. **Adaptability:** Be flexible and adaptable in your communication style to accommodate the needs and preferences of others. Adjust your approach based on the context, audience, and cultural norms to ensure effective communication and rapport.

10. **Conflict Resolution:** Use communication skills to address conflicts and disagreements constructively. Practice active listening, empathy, and assertiveness to understand the root causes of conflict and work towards mutually acceptable solutions.

By applying these effective communication techniques, individuals can enhance their interpersonal relationships, resolve conflicts, and achieve greater success in their personal, academic, and professional lives. Effective communication is a skill that can be developed and refined over time through practice, feedback, and self-awareness.

Applying Social Skills in Different Contexts

Applying social skills in different contexts involves adapting and utilizing interpersonal abilities and behaviors effectively to navigate diverse social situations. Here are examples of how social skills can be applied across various contexts:

1. **Personal Relationships:** In personal relationships, such as with family members, friends, or romantic partners, social skills are crucial for building intimacy, trust, and connection. Effective communication, active listening, empathy, and conflict resolution skills enable individuals to express themselves authentically, understand others' perspectives, and resolve disagreements constructively.

2. **Professional Settings:** In the workplace, social

skills are essential for success in various roles and industries. Strong communication skills, including verbal and written communication, facilitate effective collaboration, teamwork, and leadership. Empathy and interpersonal skills are valuable for building rapport with colleagues, clients, and stakeholders, while assertiveness and negotiation skills are important for advocating for one's ideas and interests.

3. **Academic Environments:** Social skills play a significant role in academic success, both in the classroom and in extracurricular activities. Active listening and communication skills contribute to effective participation in class discussions and group projects. Empathy and cooperation are essential for collaborating with peers, while time management and organizational skills support academic achievement and goal attainment.
4. **Community and Social Settings:** In community and social settings, such as social gatherings, clubs, or volunteer activities, social skills facilitate networking, relationship building, and community engagement. Being able to initiate and maintain conversations, demonstrate interest in others, and show respect for diverse perspectives fosters positive interactions and strengthens social connections.
5. **Online and Digital Platforms:** Social skills are increasingly important in online and digital environments, including social media platforms, forums, and virtual communities. Effective communication, digital literacy, and online etiquette enable individuals to engage positively with others, build online networks, and navigate digital interactions with integrity and respect.
6. **Cultural and Cross-Cultural Contexts:** Social

skills are also essential for navigating cultural and cross-cultural contexts, where cultural norms, values, and communication styles may vary. Cultural competence, empathy, and adaptability enable individuals to interact respectfully and effectively with people from different cultural backgrounds, fostering intercultural understanding and collaboration.

Applying social skills in different contexts requires flexibility, sensitivity, and awareness of social norms and expectations. By honing their social skills and adapting them to various situations, individuals can navigate diverse social environments with confidence, build meaningful relationships, and achieve success in their personal, academic, and professional lives.

Building Rapport and Trust

Building rapport and trust refers to the process of establishing a positive connection and mutual understanding with others, fostering a sense of comfort, respect, and confidence in the relationship. It involves creating an atmosphere of openness, authenticity, and reliability that encourages communication, collaboration, and cooperation. Building rapport and trust requires demonstrating empathy, active listening, honesty, integrity, and consistency in interactions. It is essential for fostering strong relationships, effective communication, and mutual support in personal, professional, and social contexts.

Building rapport and trust is essential for establishing strong relationships and fostering effective communication. Here are some strategies for building rapport and trust:

1. **Active Listening:** Demonstrate genuine interest in others by actively listening to their concerns, thoughts, and feelings without interruption. Use

nonverbal cues such as nodding and maintaining eye contact to show attentiveness and empathy.

2. **Empathy:** Show empathy by understanding and validating others' emotions and perspectives. Put yourself in their shoes and acknowledge their experiences with compassion and understanding.
3. **Openness and Authenticity:** Be genuine and authentic in your interactions, sharing your thoughts, feelings, and experiences openly and honestly. Avoid pretense or superficiality, and strive to establish a genuine connection based on mutual trust and respect.
4. **Respect and Courtesy:** Treat others with respect and courtesy, regardless of differences in opinion or background. Use polite language, listen without judgment, and show appreciation for their contributions and perspectives.
5. **Consistency and Reliability:** Demonstrate consistency and reliability in your actions and behavior, following through on commitments and promises. Building trust requires demonstrating integrity and reliability over time, fostering confidence in your character and intentions.
6. **Transparency:** Be transparent and forthcoming in your communication, providing clear and honest information to others. Avoid withholding information or being evasive, as this can erode trust and credibility.
7. **Empowerment:** Empower others by giving them autonomy and ownership over their decisions and actions. Trust their judgment and capabilities, and support them in achieving their goals and aspirations.
8. **Positive Communication:** Use positive language and communication to create a supportive and

uplifting atmosphere. Offer words of encouragement and affirmation, and celebrate others' achievements and successes.

9. **Boundaries and Respect:** Respect others' boundaries and personal space, and avoid crossing boundaries without their consent. Show sensitivity to their needs and preferences, and communicate with respect and consideration.

10. **Conflict Resolution:** Handle conflicts and disagreements with maturity and diplomacy, seeking mutually beneficial solutions through open communication and collaboration. Approach conflicts with empathy and a willingness to understand others' perspectives, and work towards resolution with respect and integrity.

By applying these strategies, individuals can build rapport and trust with others, creating a foundation of mutual respect and understanding in their relationships. Building rapport and trust requires ongoing effort and investment in nurturing positive connections with others, but the rewards are invaluable in fostering strong, resilient, and fulfilling relationships.

Conflict Resolution Strategies

Building rapport and trust refers to the process of establishing a positive connection and mutual understanding with others, fostering a sense of comfort, respect, and confidence in the relationship. It involves creating an atmosphere of openness, authenticity, and reliability that encourages communication, collaboration, and cooperation. Building rapport and trust requires demonstrating empathy, active listening, honesty, integrity, and consistency in interactions. It is essential for fostering strong relationships, effective communication, and mutual support in personal, professional, and social contexts.

Conflict resolution strategies refer to methods and approaches used to address and resolve conflicts or disagreements in a constructive and mutually beneficial manner. These strategies aim to de-escalate tensions, find common ground, and achieve resolution while preserving relationships and promoting understanding. Conflict resolution strategies may involve various techniques, including communication, negotiation, problem-solving, and mediation, tailored to the specific nature and context of the conflict. The goal is to facilitate a positive outcome that satisfies the interests and needs of all parties involved, fostering cooperation, collaboration, and conflict prevention in the future.

Conflict resolution strategies are methods and approaches used to manage and resolve conflicts or disagreements in a constructive and mutually beneficial manner. These strategies aim to de-escalate tensions, address underlying issues, and reach a resolution that satisfies the needs and interests of all parties involved. Here are some common conflict resolution strategies:

1. **Communication:** Open and honest communication is key to resolving conflicts. Encourage all parties to express their concerns, perspectives, and feelings without interruption. Active listening and empathetic understanding can help clarify misunderstandings and promote empathy and understanding.
2. **Negotiation:** Negotiation involves discussing differences and finding a compromise or mutually agreeable solution. Encourage parties to identify their interests and priorities, explore potential solutions collaboratively, and negotiate trade-offs or concessions as needed.
3. **Problem-Solving:** Problem-solving approaches focus on addressing the underlying issues or causes of the conflict. Encourage parties to identify

the root causes of the conflict, brainstorm potential solutions, and work together to implement effective solutions that address everyone's needs.

4. **Mediation:** Mediation involves the assistance of a neutral third party, known as a mediator, who facilitates communication and negotiation between the conflicting parties. The mediator helps parties explore their interests, communicate effectively, and reach a mutually acceptable resolution.
5. **Compromise:** Compromise entails finding a middle ground or solution that partially satisfies the interests of all parties involved. Encourage parties to identify areas of common ground and make concessions or compromises to reach an agreement that meets everyone's needs to some extent.
6. **Active Listening:** Active listening involves paying close attention to what others are saying, without interrupting or judging. Encourage parties to listen actively to each other's perspectives, clarify misunderstandings, and show empathy and understanding.
7. **Empathy:** Empathy involves understanding and acknowledging the emotions and perspectives of others. Encourage parties to consider each other's feelings, needs, and concerns, and demonstrate empathy and compassion in their interactions.
8. **Maintaining Respect:** Respect is essential for productive conflict resolution. Encourage parties to treat each other with respect and dignity, even when they disagree. Avoid personal attacks, blame, or criticism, and focus on addressing the issues constructively.

9. **Taking a Break:** Sometimes, taking a break from the conflict can help parties cool off and gain perspective. Encourage parties to take a break if emotions are running high, and reconvene when they are calmer and more ready to engage in productive dialogue.

10. **Seeking Professional Help:** In some cases, conflicts may be too complex or entrenched to resolve independently. Encourage parties to seek the assistance of a trained mediator, counselor, or conflict resolution specialist who can provide guidance and facilitate resolution.

By employing these conflict resolution strategies, parties can work together to address conflicts effectively, preserve relationships, and promote mutual understanding and cooperation.

6

Emotional Intelligence in Personal Relationships

A personal relationship refers to a close and intimate connection between two or more individuals, characterized by mutual affection, trust, and emotional bond. Unlike casual or superficial interactions, personal relationships involve a deeper level of connection, understanding, and commitment. These relationships can take various forms, including romantic partnerships, friendships, familial bonds, and close acquaintanceships. Personal relationships typically entail sharing experiences, thoughts, and feelings with each other, providing support and encouragement, and experiencing a sense of belonging and connection. They play a fundamental role in shaping individuals' emotional well-being, sense of identity, and overall quality of life. Personal relationships require effort, communication, and mutual respect to nurture and maintain, but they also offer profound benefits, including companionship, emotional support, and a sense of fulfillment and belonging.

Emotional Intelligence (EI) plays a crucial role in personal relationships, shaping how individuals perceive, understand, and interact with others on an emotional level. Here's how EI influences personal relationships:

1. **Empathy and Understanding:** EI enables individuals to empathize with their partners, understand their emotions, and respond with sensitivity and compassion. By recognizing and validating their partner's feelings, individuals can foster trust, intimacy, and connection in their relationships.
2. **Effective Communication:** EI enhances communication skills, enabling individuals to express themselves clearly, listen attentively, and communicate their needs and feelings openly and honestly. Effective communication promotes understanding, reduces misunderstandings, and strengthens the bond between partners.
3. **Conflict Resolution:** EI equips individuals with the skills needed to navigate conflicts and disagreements constructively. By remaining calm, empathizing with their partner's perspective, and communicating assertively yet respectfully, individuals can resolve conflicts and build stronger, more resilient relationships.
4. **Self-Regulation:** EI helps individuals manage their own emotions and impulses, allowing them to respond to challenging situations with patience, empathy, and understanding. By regulating their emotions effectively, individuals can avoid escalating conflicts and maintain harmony in their relationships.
5. **Building Trust:** EI fosters trust and mutual

respect in relationships by promoting honesty, integrity, and reliability. Individuals with high emotional intelligence are transparent about their feelings and intentions, communicate openly with their partners, and demonstrate consistency and reliability in their actions.

6. **Supportive Relationships:** EI contributes to the development of supportive and nurturing relationships, where partners provide emotional support, encouragement, and validation to each other. By being emotionally available and responsive, individuals can create a safe and supportive environment for their partners to thrive.

7. **Empowering Partnerships:** In emotionally intelligent relationships, partners empower each other to grow, evolve, and pursue their goals and aspirations. By providing encouragement, validation, and constructive feedback, individuals can inspire their partners to reach their full potential and achieve personal and shared goals.

8. **Resilience and Adaptability:** EI promotes resilience and adaptability in relationships, enabling partners to navigate life's ups and downs with grace and resilience. Individuals with high emotional intelligence are better equipped to weather challenges, bounce back from setbacks, and adapt to changing circumstances together.

9. **Enhanced Intimacy:** EI fosters intimacy and connection in relationships by creating a deeper understanding and emotional bond between partners. By sharing their innermost thoughts, feelings, and vulnerabilities, individuals can cultivate intimacy, trust, and closeness in their relationships.

In summary, emotional intelligence is essential for fostering healthy, fulfilling, and lasting personal relationships. By developing and honing EI skills such as empathy, communication, self-regulation, and trust-building, individuals can cultivate deeper connections, resolve conflicts, and create supportive and nurturing partnerships that thrive over time.

The Role of Emotional Intelligence in Friendships and Family

Emotional Intelligence (EI) plays a significant role in nurturing and maintaining healthy friendships and family relationships. Here's how EI influences these important aspects of our lives:

1. **Empathy and Understanding:** EI enables individuals to empathize with the feelings and experiences of their friends and family members. By understanding and validating their emotions, individuals can forge deeper connections, strengthen bonds, and offer meaningful support and encouragement.
2. **Effective Communication:** EI enhances communication skills, enabling individuals to express themselves clearly and listen attentively to their loved ones. Effective communication fosters understanding, resolves conflicts, and promotes harmony and trust in friendships and family relationships.
3. **Conflict Resolution:** EI equips individuals with the ability to navigate conflicts and disagreements constructively. By remaining calm, empathizing with others' perspectives, and communicating assertively yet respectfully, individuals can resolve conflicts and maintain positive relationships with their friends and family members.
4. **Building Trust:** EI fosters trust and mutual

respect in friendships and family relationships by promoting honesty, integrity, and reliability. Individuals with high emotional intelligence are transparent about their feelings and intentions, communicate openly, and demonstrate consistency and reliability in their actions.

5. **Support and Encouragement:** EI enables individuals to provide emotional support, encouragement, and validation to their friends and family members. By being emotionally available and responsive, individuals can create a safe and supportive environment for their loved ones to thrive and grow.
6. **Boundaries and Respect:** EI helps individuals establish and maintain healthy boundaries in their friendships and family relationships. By respecting each other's boundaries and preferences, individuals can cultivate mutual respect, trust, and understanding in their interactions.
7. **Empowering Relationships:** In emotionally intelligent relationships, friends and family members empower each other to grow, evolve, and pursue their goals and aspirations. By providing encouragement, validation, and constructive feedback, individuals can inspire their loved ones to reach their full potential and achieve personal and shared goals.
8. **Celebrating Differences:** EI encourages acceptance and appreciation of diversity in friendships and family relationships. By embracing each other's differences, individuals can foster inclusivity, respect, and understanding, enriching their relationships and deepening their connections with their loved ones.

Emotional intelligence is essential for nurturing and maintaining healthy, fulfilling, and lasting friendships and family relationships. By developing and honing EI skills such as empathy, communication, conflict resolution, and trust-building, individuals can cultivate deeper connections, resolve conflicts, and create supportive and nurturing bonds that withstand the test of time.

Building Strong, Healthy Relationships

Building strong, healthy relationships is essential for fostering happiness, fulfillment, and overall well-being. Here are some key principles and strategies for cultivating meaningful connections with others:

1. **Communication:** Effective communication is the cornerstone of any healthy relationship. This involves expressing yourself honestly and openly, actively listening to others, and being empathetic and understanding. Communication builds trust, resolves conflicts, and strengthens bonds between individuals.

2. **Trust and Honesty:** Trust is the foundation of all successful relationships. Being honest, reliable, and consistent in your words and actions fosters trust and security in your relationships. Avoiding deception, keeping promises, and being transparent builds trust and strengthens connections with others.

3. **Respect:** Respect is essential for maintaining healthy boundaries and mutual understanding in relationships. Treat others with kindness, consideration, and empathy. Acknowledge and value their opinions, feelings, and autonomy, even if they differ from your own.

4. **Empathy:** Empathy is the ability to understand and share the feelings of others. Cultivating

empathy allows you to connect with others on a deeper level, validate their experiences, and provide support and comfort when needed. Put yourself in their shoes and strive to see things from their perspective.

5. **Quality Time:** Spending quality time together is vital for building strong relationships. Make time for meaningful interactions, shared activities, and heartfelt conversations with your loved ones. Quality time fosters intimacy, strengthens connections, and creates lasting memories.
6. **Compromise and Flexibility:** Every relationship requires compromise and flexibility to accommodate each other's needs and preferences. Be willing to negotiate, make concessions, and find mutually acceptable solutions to conflicts or disagreements. Flexibility fosters cooperation, understanding, and mutual respect in relationships.
7. **Forgiveness:** Forgiveness is essential for moving past conflicts and repairing damaged relationships. Let go of grudges, resentments, and past hurts, and be willing to forgive others for their mistakes or shortcomings. Forgiveness promotes healing, reconciliation, and the restoration of trust and harmony in relationships.
8. **Support and Encouragement:** Offering support and encouragement to your loved ones strengthens your bonds and fosters a sense of connection and belonging. Be there for them during difficult times, offer a listening ear, and provide encouragement and validation. Your support can make a significant difference in their lives.
9. **Shared Values and Goals:** Shared values and

goals provide a sense of direction and purpose in relationships. Find common ground with your loved ones and work together towards shared aspirations and objectives. Shared values create unity, harmony, and a sense of partnership in relationships.

10. **Self-Care:** Taking care of yourself is crucial for building strong relationships. Prioritize your physical, emotional, and mental well-being by practicing self-care activities that recharge and rejuvenate you. When you're at your best, you can show up fully for your loved ones and contribute positively to your relationships.

By incorporating these principles and strategies into your interactions with others, you can build strong, healthy relationships that bring joy, fulfillment, and mutual support into your life. Remember that relationships require effort, patience, and nurturing, but the rewards of meaningful connections with others are immeasurable.

Managing Conflicts and Misunderstandings

Managing conflicts and misunderstandings effectively is essential for maintaining healthy relationships and promoting harmony and understanding among individuals. Here are some strategies for managing conflicts and misunderstandings:

1. **Open Communication:** Encourage open and honest communication to address conflicts and misunderstandings constructively. Create a safe and supportive environment where individuals feel comfortable expressing their thoughts, feelings, and concerns without fear of judgment or retaliation.

2. **Active Listening:** Practice active listening to understand the perspectives and emotions of

others. Listen attentively, without interrupting or formulating your response prematurely. Validate their feelings and acknowledge their experiences to demonstrate empathy and understanding.

3. **Empathy:** Put yourself in the shoes of the other person and try to understand their perspective and feelings. Empathy promotes compassion, respect, and understanding, making it easier to find common ground and resolve conflicts amicably.
4. **Clarification:** Clarify any misunderstandings or misinterpretations by seeking clarification from the other person. Ask questions to ensure that you understand their intentions, motivations, and concerns accurately. Clarification helps prevent misunderstandings from escalating into conflicts.
5. **Seek Common Ground:** Focus on areas of agreement and shared interests to find common ground with the other person. Identify common goals or objectives that both parties can work towards, fostering collaboration and cooperation in resolving conflicts.
6. **Avoid Blame and Criticism:** Refrain from blaming or criticizing the other person, as this can escalate conflicts and damage relationships. Instead, focus on addressing the issue at hand objectively and finding solutions that benefit both parties.
7. **Stay Calm and Respectful:** Manage your emotions and refrain from reacting impulsively or defensively during conflicts. Stay calm, composed, and respectful in your interactions, even if you disagree with the other person. Respectful communication fosters mutual understanding and paves the way for resolution.
8. **Find Win-Win Solutions:** Strive to find win-win

solutions that address the needs and interests of all parties involved. Be flexible and willing to compromise to reach a mutually acceptable resolution that satisfies everyone's concerns.

9. **Take a Break if Necessary:** If emotions are running high or the conflict seems unproductive, consider taking a break to cool off and regain perspective. A temporary pause can help individuals approach the conflict with a clearer mind and a renewed sense of calm.
10. **Seek Mediation if Needed:** If conflicts persist despite your efforts to resolve them, consider seeking the assistance of a neutral third party, such as a mediator or counselor, to facilitate communication and negotiation. Mediation can help parties explore underlying issues, generate creative solutions, and reach a mutually agreeable resolution.

By implementing these strategies, individuals can manage conflicts and misunderstandings effectively, promote mutual understanding and respect, and strengthen relationships based on trust, empathy, and cooperation. Conflict resolution is an ongoing process that requires patience, empathy, and a willingness to work towards mutually beneficial solutions.

Exercises for Enhancing Emotional Intelligence in Personal Relationships

Enhancing emotional intelligence (EI) in personal relationships involves practicing skills such as empathy, communication, and self-awareness. Here are some exercises that can help individuals improve their EI in their relationships:

1. **Journaling:** Encourage individuals to keep a journal where they can reflect on their thoughts, feelings, and interactions with others. Writing

about their experiences can enhance self-awareness and emotional insight, helping them better understand their own emotions and behaviors.

2. **Emotion Labeling:** Practice identifying and labeling emotions in oneself and others. Use emotion words to describe feelings and discuss how they impact behavior and relationships. This exercise promotes emotional awareness and empathy, enhancing communication and understanding in relationships.

3. **Active Listening:** Practice active listening skills by having individuals engage in conversations where they focus on fully understanding the other person's perspective without interrupting or judging. Encourage them to paraphrase and summarize what the other person is saying to demonstrate understanding and empathy.

4. **Empathy Exercises:** Engage in empathy-building exercises where individuals put themselves in the shoes of others and imagine how they might feel in a given situation. This can involve role-playing scenarios or discussing hypothetical situations to develop empathy and understanding for others' experiences.

5. **Conflict Resolution Role-Play:** Role-play conflict resolution scenarios where individuals practice using EI skills such as active listening, empathy, and problem-solving to resolve conflicts effectively. Encourage them to experiment with different approaches and strategies for managing conflicts and finding mutually satisfactory solutions.

6. **Self-Reflection:** Encourage individuals to engage in regular self-reflection practices, such as mindfulness meditation or quiet contemplation.

This allows them to become more aware of their thoughts, feelings, and reactions, fostering greater self-awareness and emotional regulation in their relationships.

7. **Gratitude Practice:** Cultivate gratitude by encouraging individuals to express appreciation for the people in their lives. This can involve keeping a gratitude journal, writing thank-you notes, or simply verbally expressing gratitude to loved ones. Practicing gratitude enhances positive emotions and strengthens interpersonal connections.
8. **Assertiveness Training:** Help individuals develop assertiveness skills by teaching them how to express their thoughts, feelings, and needs confidently and respectfully. Role-play assertive communication scenarios and provide feedback on their communication style and effectiveness.
9. **Boundary Setting:** Practice setting and maintaining healthy boundaries in relationships. Encourage individuals to identify their boundaries and communicate them clearly and assertively to others. This helps prevent resentment and conflict by ensuring that individuals' needs and limits are respected.
10. **Relationship Check-Ins:** Regularly check in with individuals about their relationships and emotional well-being. This can involve discussing challenges, successes, and areas for growth in their relationships and providing support and guidance as needed.

By incorporating these exercises into their daily lives, individuals can enhance their emotional intelligence and cultivate healthier, more fulfilling relationships with others. Practicing EI skills regularly can lead to greater empathy, communication, and connection in personal relationships, contributing to overall happiness and well-being.

Emotional Check-Ins

Emotional check-ins refer to the practice of regularly assessing and monitoring one's own emotional state. This process involves taking the time to pause, reflect, and tune into one's feelings and emotions, with the goal of increasing self-awareness and promoting emotional well-being. Emotional check-ins can be conducted individually or as part of a structured activity or practice, such as journaling, meditation, or therapy sessions.

The purpose of emotional check-ins is to cultivate mindfulness and self-awareness, allowing individuals to become more attuned to their emotions, thoughts, and bodily sensations. By checking in with themselves regularly, individuals can gain insight into their emotional patterns, triggers, and responses, which can help them better understand and manage their emotions in various situations.

Emotional check-ins often involve asking oneself questions such as:

- "How am I feeling right now?"
- "What emotions am I experiencing?"
- "What thoughts are running through my mind?"
- "Are there any physical sensations associated with my emotions?"
- "What might have triggered these emotions?"
- "How can I best support myself in this moment?"

Through the practice of emotional check-ins, individuals can develop greater emotional intelligence, resilience, and self-regulation skills. They can learn to recognize and acknowledge their emotions without judgment, respond to them in healthy and constructive ways, and cultivate a greater sense of balance and well-being in their lives. Emotional check-ins also provide an opportunity for individuals to check in with their needs and take proactive steps to prioritize self-care and self-compassion. Overall, emotional check-ins serve as a valuable tool for promoting self-awareness, emotional wellness, and personal growth. Emotional check-ins are structured practices designed to help individuals assess and regulate their emotions regularly. These check-ins involve reflecting on one's emotional state, identifying any underlying feelings or triggers, and implementing strategies to manage emotions effectively. Here is how to conduct emotional check-ins:

1. **Set Aside Time:** Schedule regular intervals, such as daily, weekly, or monthly, to conduct emotional check-ins. Choose a time when you can dedicate uninterrupted focus to reflect on your emotions.
2. **Create a Safe Space:** Find a quiet and comfortable environment where you can engage in self-reflection without distractions. This could be a private room, a peaceful outdoor setting, or any space where you feel calm and relaxed.
3. **Reflect on Emotions:** Begin by tuning into your emotional state and identifying how you're feeling in the present moment. Use emotion words to label your feelings, such as happy, sad, anxious, or angry. Be honest with yourself about your emotions, acknowledging both positive and negative feelings.
4. **Explore Triggers:** Reflect on any events, situations, or interactions that may have influenced your emotional state. Consider what triggered your emotions and how you responded to these triggers. This self-awareness helps you understand your emotional reactions and patterns.

5. **Practice Mindfulness:** Engage in mindfulness techniques, such as deep breathing, meditation, or body scans, to center yourself and cultivate present-moment awareness. Mindfulness helps you observe your thoughts and feelings without judgment, promoting emotional regulation and clarity.

6. **Check-In with Physical Sensations:** Pay attention to any physical sensations associated with your emotions, such as tension in your body, changes in your heart rate, or sensations in your stomach. Physical cues can provide valuable insight into your emotional state and help you manage stress and tension.

7. **Identify Coping Strategies:** Once you've identified your emotions and triggers, brainstorm coping strategies to manage difficult emotions effectively. This could involve relaxation techniques, problem-solving strategies, seeking support from others, or engaging in enjoyable activities that uplift your mood.

8. **Set Intentions:** Determine how you want to navigate your emotions moving forward. Set intentions or goals for how you'll respond to challenging situations or emotions in a more constructive and adaptive way. Focus on cultivating resilience, self-compassion, and emotional well-being.

9. **Track Progress:** Keep a journal or record of your emotional check-ins to track your progress over time. Note any patterns or changes in your emotional responses, as well as the effectiveness of different coping strategies. Reflect on what you've learned and adjust your approach as needed.

10. **Seek Support if Necessary:** If you're struggling to manage your emotions or find effective coping strategies, don't hesitate to seek support from a trusted friend, family member, or mental health professional. Talking to others can provide valuable perspective, validation, and encouragement.

Emotional check-ins are valuable tools for promoting self-awareness, emotional regulation, and well-being. By making them a regular part of your routine, you can develop greater resilience, self-understanding, and emotional balance in your daily life.

Practicing Gratitude and Appreciation

one's life, whether they are tangible (such as material possessions or achievements) or intangible (such as relationships, experiences, or moments of joy). Gratitude often involves a sense of humility and recognition that one's well-being and happiness are influenced by factors beyond one's control, such as the actions of others, the beauty of nature, or moments of serendipity.

Appreciation, on the other hand, generally refers to the recognition and admiration of the qualities, efforts, or contributions of someone or something. It involves valuing and acknowledging the positive aspects or benefits that someone or something brings to one's life. Appreciation can be directed towards individuals, such as friends, family members, colleagues, or mentors, for their kindness, support, or talents. It can also be directed towards experiences, such as moments of beauty, inspiration, or personal growth, or towards objects, such as works of art, music, or literature, for their aesthetic or emotional value.

In essence, gratitude and appreciation both involve recognizing and valuing the positive aspects of life, whether they come from external sources or are cultivated within oneself. They are attitudes or mindsets that can enhance well-being, foster positive relationships, and cultivate a greater sense of happiness, contentment, and fulfillment in life. By practicing gratitude and appreciation regularly, individuals can cultivate a more positive outlook, deepen their connections with others, and enhance their overall quality of life. Practicing gratitude and appreciation is a powerful way to cultivate positivity, enhance well-being, and strengthen relationships. Here are some strategies for incorporating gratitude into your daily life:

1. **Gratitude Journaling:** Set aside time each day to write down things you're grateful for. Focus on specific moments, experiences, or people that have brought joy, comfort, or meaning to your life. Reflect on why you're grateful for these things and how they've enriched your life.

2. **Expressing Appreciation:** Take the time to express gratitude and appreciation to others. Tell your loved ones how much you value and appreciate them, whether through verbal expressions, handwritten notes, or thoughtful gestures. Acknowledge their kindness, support, and contributions to your life.

3. **Mindful Gratitude Practice:** Incorporate gratitude into your mindfulness or meditation practice. During moments of stillness and reflection, focus on feelings of gratitude and appreciation for the present moment, your surroundings, and the people in your life. Cultivate a sense of awe and wonder for the beauty and abundance around you.

4. **Gratitude Rituals:** Create rituals or routines that remind you to practice gratitude regularly. This could involve starting or ending each day with a gratitude meditation, sharing gratitudes around

the dinner table with your family, or keeping a gratitude jar where you collect notes of appreciation throughout the year.

5. **Gratitude Walks:** Take mindful walks outdoors and observe the beauty of nature around you. Notice the sights, sounds, and sensations of the natural world, and reflect on the abundance and wonder it offers. Use this time to cultivate feelings of gratitude and connection with the world around you.
6. **Gratitude Challenges:** Participate in gratitude challenges or initiatives that encourage you to focus on gratitude daily. This could involve joining online gratitude challenges, using gratitude apps or journals, or participating in community gratitude events. Challenge yourself to find something to be grateful for each day, no matter how small.
7. **Counting Blessings:** Create a "blessings list" where you write down all the things you're grateful for in your life. This can include material possessions, relationships, opportunities, experiences, and personal qualities. Refer to your blessings list regularly to remind yourself of the abundance and richness in your life.
8. **Gratitude in Adversity:** Practice finding gratitude even in challenging or difficult situations. Look for silver linings, lessons learned, or opportunities for growth and resilience. Cultivating gratitude in adversity can help shift your perspective and empower you to navigate challenges with grace and optimism.
9. **Random Acts of Kindness:** Spread gratitude and appreciation by performing random acts of kindness for others. Whether it's complimenting

a stranger, offering assistance to someone in need, or performing a thoughtful gesture for a friend or coworker, acts of kindness can foster gratitude and connection in both giver and receiver.

10. **Reflecting on Gratitude:** Take time to reflect on the positive effects of gratitude in your life. Notice how practicing gratitude enhances your mood, relationships, and overall well-being. Celebrate the transformative power of gratitude and commit to making it a lifelong practice.

By incorporating these strategies into your daily life, you can cultivate a deeper sense of gratitude and appreciation for the abundance and beauty that surrounds you. Practicing gratitude regularly can enhance your overall happiness, resilience, and quality of life, while also strengthening your relationships and fostering a greater sense of connection with others.

7

Emotional Intelligence in the Workplace

Emotional Intelligence (EI) has become increasingly recognized as a crucial factor in workplace success and effectiveness. Defined as the ability to recognize, understand, and manage one's own emotions, as well as to recognize, understand, and influence the emotions of others, EI plays a significant role in various aspects of the workplace, from leadership and teamwork to customer relations and organizational culture. Here are some key ways in which EI impacts the workplace:

1. **Leadership Effectiveness:** Leaders with high emotional intelligence are better equipped to inspire, motivate, and engage their teams. They possess strong interpersonal skills, such as empathy, active listening, and effective communication, which enable them to connect with their employees on a deeper level and foster trust and collaboration. EI helps leaders navigate

complex interpersonal dynamics, resolve conflicts, and make decisions that consider both the needs of the organization and the well-being of its employees.

2. **Teamwork and Collaboration:** EI contributes to the effectiveness of teamwork and collaboration by promoting positive relationships and communication among team members. Individuals with high emotional intelligence are better able to understand and appreciate the perspectives and contributions of their colleagues, leading to improved cooperation, coordination, and synergy within teams. EI also helps teams navigate conflicts and disagreements constructively, fostering a culture of respect, trust, and mutual support.

3. **Conflict Resolution:** EI skills such as empathy, communication, and emotional regulation are essential for managing conflicts and disagreements in the workplace. Individuals with high emotional intelligence are able to remain calm under pressure, listen actively to others' perspectives, and find mutually satisfactory solutions to conflicts. By addressing conflicts with sensitivity and understanding, rather than defensiveness or aggression, EI promotes a positive work environment and preserves relationships among colleagues.

4. **Customer Relations:** EI is critical for building rapport, understanding customer needs and preferences, and delivering exceptional service. Frontline employees who possess strong emotional intelligence can effectively manage customer interactions, handle complaints or difficult situations with grace and empathy, and build long-lasting relationships with customers based

on trust and satisfaction. EI also enables employees to adapt their communication style and approach to meet the diverse needs of customers, leading to improved customer loyalty and retention.

5. **Decision-Making:** EI influences decision-making by helping individuals consider both rational and emotional factors when evaluating options. Leaders and employees who are emotionally intelligent are better able to anticipate the potential impact of decisions on themselves and others, as well as to manage their own biases and emotions throughout the decision-making process. By making decisions that are informed by empathy, intuition, and social awareness, rather than solely by logic or reason, individuals can make choices that are more aligned with organizational goals and values.

6. **Stress Management:** EI skills such as self-awareness, self-regulation, and resilience are essential for managing stress and pressure in the workplace. Employees who are emotionally intelligent are better equipped to recognize the signs of stress in themselves and others, as well as to implement coping strategies to reduce stress and maintain well-being. By fostering a culture that values self-care, work-life balance, and psychological safety, organizations can support employees in managing stress effectively and performing at their best.

7. **Organizational Culture:** EI contributes to the development of a positive organizational culture characterized by trust, respect, and collaboration. When leaders and employees demonstrate high levels of emotional intelligence, they set a positive example for others and create a work environment

where individuals feel valued, supported, and motivated to contribute their best efforts. Organizations that prioritize EI in their hiring, training, and development initiatives are more likely to attract and retain top talent, as well as to achieve greater employee engagement, satisfaction, and loyalty.

Emotional Intelligence plays a critical role in the workplace by influencing leadership effectiveness, teamwork and collaboration, conflict resolution, customer relations, decision-making, stress management, and organizational culture. By developing and nurturing EI skills among leaders and employees, organizations can create a more positive and productive work environment, enhance employee well-being and satisfaction, and ultimately achieve greater success and competitiveness in today's complex and dynamic business landscape.

Importance of Emotional Intelligence in Professional Settings

Emotional Intelligence (EI) holds significant importance in professional settings due to its profound impact on various aspects of workplace dynamics, employee performance, and organizational success. Here are several reasons why EI is crucial in professional environments:

1. **Effective Leadership:** Leaders with high EI possess the interpersonal skills necessary to inspire, motivate, and influence others effectively. They excel in areas such as communication, empathy, and relationship-building, enabling them to foster trust, collaboration, and engagement among their team members. EI helps leaders navigate complex interpersonal dynamics, resolve conflicts, and adapt their leadership style to meet the diverse needs of their employees.

2. **Teamwork and Collaboration:** EI promotes positive relationships and communication among team members, leading to improved teamwork and collaboration. Individuals with high EI are better able to understand and appreciate the perspectives, strengths, and contributions of their colleagues, fostering a culture of respect, trust, and mutual support within teams. EI also helps teams navigate conflicts and disagreements constructively, leading to more effective problem-solving and decision-making.

3. **Customer Relations:** In customer-facing roles, EI is critical for building rapport, understanding customer needs, and delivering exceptional service. Employees with high EI can effectively manage customer interactions, handle complaints or difficult situations with empathy and professionalism, and build strong relationships with customers based on trust and satisfaction. EI enables employees to adapt their communication style and approach to meet the diverse needs of customers, leading to improved customer loyalty and retention.

4. **Conflict Resolution:** EI skills such as empathy, communication, and emotional regulation are essential for managing conflicts and disagreements in the workplace. Individuals with high EI can remain calm under pressure, listen actively to others' perspectives, and find mutually satisfactory solutions to conflicts. By addressing conflicts with sensitivity and understanding, rather than defensiveness or aggression, EI promotes a positive work environment and preserves relationships among colleagues.

5. **Decision-Making:** EI influences decision-making by helping individuals consider both rational and

emotional factors when evaluating options. Professionals with high EI are better able to anticipate the potential impact of decisions on themselves and others, as well as to manage their own biases and emotions throughout the decision-making process. By making decisions that are informed by empathy, intuition, and social awareness, individuals can make choices that are more aligned with organizational goals and values.

6. **Stress Management:** EI skills such as self-awareness, self-regulation, and resilience are essential for managing stress and pressure in the workplace. Employees with high EI can recognize the signs of stress in themselves and others, as well as implement coping strategies to reduce stress and maintain well-being. By fostering a culture that values self-care, work-life balance, and psychological safety, organizations can support employees in managing stress effectively and performing at their best.

7. **Organizational Culture:** EI contributes to the development of a positive organizational culture characterized by trust, respect, and collaboration. When leaders and employees demonstrate high levels of emotional intelligence, they set a positive example for others and create a work environment where individuals feel valued, supported, and motivated to contribute their best efforts. Organizations that prioritize EI in their hiring, training, and development initiatives are more likely to attract and retain top talent, as well as achieve greater employee engagement, satisfaction, and loyalty.

In summary, Emotional Intelligence is crucial in professional settings because it enhances leadership effectiveness, teamwork and collaboration, customer relations, conflict resolution, decision-making, stress management, and organizational culture. By developing and nurturing EI skills among leaders and employees, organizations can create a more positive and productive work environment, enhance employee well-being and satisfaction, and ultimately achieve greater success and competitiveness in today's dynamic business landscape.

Enhancing Leadership Skills

Leadership skills refer to the abilities, qualities, and competencies that enable individuals to effectively lead, inspire, and influence others towards a common goal or objective. These skills encompass a wide range of traits and behaviors that are essential for guiding and motivating individuals or teams to achieve success in various settings, including the workplace, community organizations, and personal relationships. Leadership skills can be categorized into several key areas:

1. **Communication:** Effective communication is fundamental to leadership. Leaders must be able to articulate their vision, goals, and expectations clearly and concisely to their team members. They should also be skilled listeners, capable of actively listening to the ideas, concerns, and feedback of others and fostering open and honest dialogue.

2. **Decision-Making:** Leaders must possess strong decision-making skills to make timely and well-informed decisions that align with the organization's goals and values. This includes gathering relevant information, evaluating alternatives, considering potential risks and consequences, and making decisive choices.

3. **Problem-Solving:** Leaders are often faced with complex challenges and obstacles that require creative and strategic problem-solving skills. They must be able to analyze problems, identify root

causes, generate innovative solutions, and implement effective action plans to address issues and achieve desired outcomes.

4. **Emotional Intelligence:** Emotional intelligence (EI) is crucial for effective leadership. Leaders with high EI are able to understand and manage their own emotions, as well as those of others. They possess empathy, self-awareness, and social skills that enable them to build strong relationships, resolve conflicts, and inspire trust and collaboration.
5. **Adaptability:** In today's rapidly changing world, leaders must be adaptable and flexible to navigate uncertainty and change effectively. They should be able to adjust their plans, strategies, and approaches in response to evolving circumstances and unexpected challenges while remaining focused on achieving their goals.
6. **Vision and Strategic Planning:** Successful leaders have a clear vision for the future and the ability to develop and communicate a compelling strategy to achieve that vision. They set ambitious yet achievable goals, establish priorities, and create actionable plans to drive progress and organizational growth.
7. **Team Building and Motivation:** Leaders must be skilled at building and motivating high-performing teams. They should be able to recruit, develop, and empower talented individuals, foster a culture of collaboration and trust, and inspire team members to work towards shared goals with enthusiasm and dedication.
8. **Delegation:** Effective leaders know how to delegate tasks and responsibilities appropriately, leveraging the strengths and expertise of their

team members. They empower others to take ownership of projects, encourage autonomy and accountability, and provide support and guidance as needed.

9. **Conflict Resolution:** Leaders must be adept at managing conflicts and disagreements within their teams or organizations. They should be able to facilitate constructive dialogue, mediate disputes, and find mutually acceptable solutions that preserve relationships and promote unity and cooperation.
10. **Ethical Leadership:** Integrity and ethics are essential qualities of effective leadership. Leaders must demonstrate honesty, transparency, and ethical behavior in all their interactions and decisions, inspiring trust and confidence among their team members and stakeholders.

Leadership skills are not innate but can be developed and refined through education, training, and experience. By continually honing their skills in these key areas, individuals can enhance their leadership effectiveness and make a positive impact in their organizations and communities.

Enhancing leadership skills is an ongoing process that involves self-awareness, continuous learning, and intentional practice. Here are some strategies to help individuals improve and develop their leadership abilities:

1. **Self-Reflection:** Take time to reflect on your strengths, weaknesses, values, and leadership style. Consider past experiences, successes, and challenges, and identify areas for growth and improvement. Self-reflection promotes self-awareness, which is essential for effective leadership.
2. **Set Clear Goals:** Establish clear, achievable goals

for your leadership development journey. Identify specific areas you want to improve, such as communication, decision-making, or conflict resolution, and create a plan to work towards those goals.

3. **Seek Feedback:** Solicit feedback from colleagues, mentors, and team members about your leadership style and performance. Be open to constructive criticism and use feedback as an opportunity for growth and development. Actively listen to others' perspectives and consider how you can apply their feedback to improve your leadership skills.
4. **Continuous Learning:** Commit to lifelong learning and professional development. Attend leadership seminars, workshops, or training programs to expand your knowledge and skills. Stay up-to-date on industry trends, best practices, and emerging leadership theories to remain relevant and effective as a leader.
5. **Lead by Example:** Demonstrate the behaviors and qualities you want to see in others. Lead by example by exhibiting integrity, accountability, and resilience in your actions and decisions. Model the values and principles you want your team to uphold, and inspire others through your words and actions.
6. **Develop Emotional Intelligence:** Cultivate emotional intelligence by enhancing your self-awareness, self-regulation, empathy, and social skills. Recognize and understand your own emotions and those of others, and learn to manage them effectively in various situations. Emotional intelligence is essential for building strong relationships, fostering trust, and leading with empathy and authenticity.

7. **Empower Others:** Foster a culture of empowerment and trust within your team by delegating tasks, providing opportunities for growth and development, and recognizing and appreciating their contributions. Encourage autonomy, creativity, and initiative among team members, and support them in achieving their goals and aspirations.

8. **Effective Communication:** Enhance your communication skills by practicing active listening, clarity, and empathy. Communicate your vision, expectations, and goals clearly and effectively to your team, and encourage open and honest dialogue. Be approachable and accessible to your team members, and foster a culture of transparency and collaboration.

9. **Build Relationships:** Invest time and effort in building strong relationships with your team members, colleagues, and stakeholders. Get to know them on a personal level, show genuine interest and care for their well-being, and provide support and mentorship as needed. Building trust and rapport is essential for effective leadership and teamwork.

10. **Adaptability:** Develop adaptability and flexibility to navigate change and uncertainty effectively. Be open to new ideas, perspectives, and approaches, and be willing to adapt your leadership style to meet the evolving needs of your team and organization. Embrace challenges as opportunities for growth and innovation, and lead your team with resilience and agility.

By implementing these strategies and committing to continuous growth and development, individuals can enhance their leadership skills and become more effective, inspiring, and influential leaders in their organizations and communities. Leadership is a journey of self-discovery and growth, and by investing in their development, individuals can unlock their full potential and make a positive impact in the world.

Fostering Teamwork and Collaboration

Fostering teamwork and collaboration refers to creating an environment where individuals work together effectively towards a common goal, leveraging each other's strengths and perspectives to achieve shared objectives. It involves promoting open communication, mutual respect, and collective problem-solving among team members, with the aim of maximizing productivity, creativity, and overall team performance.

At its core, fostering teamwork and collaboration involves:

1. **Building Relationships:** Encouraging team members to build strong relationships based on trust, respect, and mutual support. This involves getting to know one another on a personal level, understanding each other's strengths and weaknesses, and developing a sense of camaraderie and cohesion within the team.
2. **Effective Communication:** Establishing clear channels of communication to ensure that information flows freely among team members. This includes promoting open and honest dialogue, active listening, and providing feedback in a constructive manner. Effective communication helps prevent misunderstandings, resolves conflicts, and fosters a shared understanding of goals and expectations.
3. **Clarifying Goals and Roles:** Clearly defining team goals, objectives, and individual roles and responsibilities is essential for promoting teamwork and collaboration. When everyone

understands what is expected of them and how their contributions align with the team's objectives, they are more likely to work together cohesively towards achieving common goals.

4. **Encouraging Diversity and Inclusion:** Embracing diversity and inclusion within the team by valuing and respecting the unique perspectives, backgrounds, and experiences of all team members. A diverse team brings a variety of viewpoints and ideas to the table, which can lead to more innovative solutions and better decision-making.
5. **Promoting Problem-Solving and Decision-Making:** Encouraging team members to collaborate on problem-solving and decision-making processes fosters a sense of ownership and accountability within the team. By involving everyone in the decision-making process and considering different viewpoints, teams can arrive at more well-rounded and effective solutions.
6. **Providing Support and Recognition:** Offering support, encouragement, and recognition to team members for their contributions and achievements is crucial for fostering a positive team environment. When team members feel valued and appreciated for their efforts, they are more likely to remain motivated and engaged in their work.
7. **Leading by Example:** As a leader or manager, leading by example is essential for fostering teamwork and collaboration within the team. Demonstrating collaborative behavior, promoting a culture of transparency and accountability, and actively participating in team activities and discussions sets a positive tone and encourages others to follow suit.

Overall, fostering teamwork and collaboration is about creating an environment where individuals feel empowered to work together towards shared goals, leveraging each other's strengths and expertise to achieve success. When teams collaborate effectively, they are better equipped to overcome challenges, capitalize on opportunities, and achieve greater results than individuals working in isolation.

Fostering teamwork and collaboration is essential for achieving organizational success and maximizing the potential of individual team members. Here are several strategies for promoting a collaborative and cohesive team environment:

1. **Establish a Shared Vision:** Clearly articulate the team's mission, goals, and objectives to ensure that everyone is aligned and working towards a common purpose. Encourage team members to contribute their ideas and perspectives to shape the vision and create a sense of ownership and commitment.
2. **Build Trust:** Trust is the foundation of effective teamwork. Foster trust among team members by being transparent, reliable, and respectful in your interactions. Encourage open communication, active listening, and mutual support to create a safe and supportive environment where individuals feel comfortable sharing their ideas and opinions.
3. **Encourage Diversity and Inclusion:** Embrace diversity and inclusion within the team by valuing and respecting the unique backgrounds, experiences, and perspectives of all team members. Recognize the strengths and contributions that each individual brings to the team and create opportunities for collaboration and learning across different backgrounds and perspectives.

4. **Promote Communication:** Communication is key to effective collaboration. Establish clear channels of communication and encourage open and honest dialogue among team members. Foster a culture where feedback is welcomed and encouraged, and ensure that everyone has the opportunity to express their ideas, concerns, and feedback.
5. **Clarify Roles and Responsibilities:** Clearly define roles, responsibilities, and expectations for each team member to avoid confusion and conflicts. Ensure that everyone understands their contribution to the team's goals and how their work aligns with the broader objectives of the organization.
6. **Facilitate Team Building Activities:** Organize team-building activities and exercises to strengthen relationships, build rapport, and foster camaraderie among team members. These activities can range from informal social gatherings to structured team-building workshops or retreats designed to promote collaboration, trust, and teamwork.
7. **Encourage Collaboration:** Create opportunities for collaboration and teamwork by assigning projects or tasks that require cooperation and collective problem-solving. Encourage cross-functional collaboration by bringing together individuals with diverse skills and expertise to tackle complex challenges and drive innovation.
8. **Provide Resources and Support:** Ensure that team members have access to the resources, tools, and support they need to succeed in their roles. Provide training, mentorship, and development opportunities to help individuals build their skills and confidence, and offer guidance and support as needed to overcome obstacles and achieve their goals.

9. **Celebrate Achievements:** Recognize and celebrate the achievements and milestones of the team as a whole and individual team members. Acknowledge their contributions and efforts, and publicly praise their successes to reinforce a culture of appreciation and recognition within the team.
10. **Lead by Example:** As a leader or manager, lead by example by demonstrating collaborative behavior and promoting a teamwork-oriented culture. Encourage collaboration, cooperation, and inclusivity in your own actions and decisions, and serve as a role model for others to emulate.

By implementing these strategies and fostering a culture of teamwork and collaboration, organizations can harness the collective talents and strengths of their teams to achieve greater innovation, productivity, and success. A collaborative team environment not only enhances job satisfaction and morale but also drives organizational growth and competitiveness in today's dynamic business landscape.

Strategies for Applying Emotional Intelligence at Work

Applying emotional intelligence (EI) at work involves leveraging one's ability to recognize, understand, and manage emotions effectively in various professional situations. Here are several strategies for applying EI in the workplace:

1. **Self-Awareness:** Start by developing self-awareness, which involves recognizing your own emotions, strengths, weaknesses, and triggers. Pay attention to how you feel in different situations and how your emotions influence your thoughts, behaviors, and interactions with others. By understanding your own emotional responses,

you can better manage them and respond more effectively in challenging situations.

2. **Emotional Regulation:** Practice emotional regulation techniques to manage your emotions in the workplace. This includes techniques such as deep breathing, mindfulness, and positive self-talk to calm yourself down when feeling stressed, anxious, or upset. By learning to regulate your emotions, you can maintain composure, make clearer decisions, and handle conflicts or pressure situations more effectively.

3. **Empathy:** Cultivate empathy towards your colleagues, clients, and stakeholders by putting yourself in their shoes and understanding their perspectives, feelings, and concerns. Listen actively, validate their emotions, and show genuine concern and understanding for their experiences. Empathy fosters trust, rapport, and collaboration in professional relationships and enables you to communicate more effectively with others.

4. **Effective Communication:** Improve your communication skills to convey your thoughts, ideas, and feedback clearly and empathetically. Use active listening techniques to understand others' viewpoints and respond thoughtfully and respectfully. Tailor your communication style and approach to the preferences and needs of your audience, whether it's your team, clients, or superiors.

5. **Conflict Resolution:** Develop conflict resolution skills to navigate disagreements and conflicts constructively in the workplace. Approach conflicts with empathy, openness, and a willingness to find mutually beneficial solutions. Practice active listening, seek common ground,

and focus on addressing underlying concerns rather than assigning blame or escalating tensions.

6. **Building Relationships:** Invest in building strong, positive relationships with your colleagues, clients, and stakeholders. Demonstrate authenticity, trustworthiness, and respect in your interactions, and take the time to get to know others on a personal level. Building rapport and trust fosters collaboration, teamwork, and mutual support, leading to better outcomes and a more positive work environment.

7. **Adaptability:** Cultivate adaptability and flexibility to navigate change and uncertainty in the workplace. Embrace new challenges, learn from setbacks, and remain open to feedback and constructive criticism. By adapting to changing circumstances with resilience and optimism, you can maintain productivity and effectiveness in the face of adversity.

8. **Leadership:** Apply emotional intelligence principles to your leadership style to inspire and motivate your team members. Lead by example by demonstrating self-awareness, empathy, and emotional regulation in your actions and decisions. Foster a culture of trust, collaboration, and open communication within your team, and empower others to reach their full potential.

9. **Feedback and Growth:** Seek feedback from others on your emotional intelligence skills and areas for improvement. Actively solicit input from colleagues, mentors, or coaches, and use their feedback to identify opportunities for growth and development. Continuously strive to enhance your emotional intelligence skills through self-reflection, learning, and practice.

10. **Work-Life Balance:** Prioritize work-life balance and self-care to maintain your overall well-being and emotional resilience. Set boundaries between work and personal life, prioritize activities that recharge and rejuvenate you, and seek support from friends, family, or professional resources when needed. Balancing your emotional needs with your professional responsibilities allows you to perform at your best and sustain long-term success in your career.

By applying these strategies for emotional intelligence at work, you can enhance your effectiveness, productivity, and satisfaction in your professional role while fostering positive relationships and a supportive work environment for yourself and others.

Navigating Workplace Conflicts

Workplace conflicts refer to disagreements, disputes, or tensions that arise between individuals or groups within an organization. These conflicts can occur due to differences in perspectives, values, interests, or goals, as well as misunderstandings, communication breakdowns, or competition for resources or recognition. Workplace conflicts can manifest in various forms, including interpersonal conflicts between colleagues, conflicts between managers and employees, or conflicts stemming from organizational changes or policies.

Conflict in the workplace is a natural and inevitable aspect of organizational dynamics, as individuals with diverse backgrounds, experiences, and personalities come together to collaborate and achieve common goals. While some conflicts may arise from interpersonal differences or misunderstandings, others may stem from structural or systemic issues within the organization, such as unclear roles or responsibilities, lack of resources, or poor communication channels.

While workplace conflicts can sometimes be disruptive or challenging to manage, they also present opportunities for growth, learning, and organizational improvement. When handled constructively, conflicts can lead to increased creativity, innovation, and collaboration, as individuals or groups work together to find mutually beneficial solutions to their differences.

However, if left unresolved or mismanaged, workplace conflicts can escalate, leading to decreased morale, productivity, and job satisfaction, as well as damaged relationships and increased turnover. Therefore, it is essential for organizations to address conflicts proactively and provide employees with the tools, resources, and support they need to navigate conflicts effectively.

Overall, workplace conflicts are a normal part of organizational life, and how they are managed can have a significant impact on employee engagement, team dynamics, and organizational performance. By promoting open communication, empathy, and constructive conflict resolution strategies, organizations can create a positive and supportive work environment where conflicts are addressed respectfully and resolved in a manner that fosters collaboration and mutual understanding.

Navigating workplace conflicts effectively is essential for maintaining a positive and productive work environment. Here are some strategies for handling conflicts constructively:

1. **Address the Issue Early:** Deal with conflicts as soon as they arise rather than letting them escalate. Addressing issues promptly prevents them from festering and becoming more challenging to resolve.
2. **Stay Calm and Professional:** Maintain your composure and professionalism when addressing

conflicts. Avoid reacting emotionally or getting defensive, as this can escalate tensions and hinder productive communication.

3. **Listen Actively:** Practice active listening to understand the perspectives and concerns of all parties involved in the conflict. Listen without interrupting, validate their feelings, and demonstrate empathy to build rapport and trust.
4. **Clarify Misunderstandings:** Often, conflicts arise from misunderstandings or miscommunication. Clarify any misunderstandings by paraphrasing what you've heard and asking clarifying questions to ensure that everyone is on the same page.
5. **Focus on Interests, Not Positions:** Encourage parties to focus on their underlying interests rather than their positions. Help them identify their needs, concerns, and goals and explore mutually beneficial solutions that address everyone's interests.
6. **Seek Common Ground:** Look for areas of agreement or common ground between parties as a starting point for resolution. Finding shared interests or goals can help build rapport and facilitate compromise.
7. **Generate Solutions Together:** Collaborate with the parties involved to brainstorm potential solutions to the conflict. Encourage creativity and open-mindedness and explore different options to find a resolution that meets everyone's needs.
8. **Use Assertive Communication:** Assertively communicate your own needs, concerns, and boundaries while also respecting those of others. Use "I" statements to express yourself non-defensively and assert your perspective without blaming or criticizing others.

9. **Manage Emotions:** Help parties manage their emotions during conflict resolution by encouraging emotional regulation techniques such as deep breathing, taking breaks, or reframing negative thoughts. Create a safe space for expressing emotions while maintaining a focus on problem-solving and constructive dialogue.
10. **Explore Third-Party Mediation:** If conflicts persist or become too complex to resolve independently, consider seeking the assistance of a neutral third party, such as a mediator or HR professional. Mediators can facilitate communication, manage power imbalances, and help parties find mutually acceptable solutions.
11. **Follow Up:** After reaching a resolution, follow up with the parties involved to ensure that the agreed-upon solutions are implemented effectively. Monitor the situation closely and address any issues or concerns that may arise promptly.
12. **Learn from the Conflict:** Encourage parties to reflect on the conflict and identify lessons learned or areas for improvement. Use conflicts as opportunities for growth and learning to strengthen relationships and prevent similar issues from arising in the future.

By employing these strategies for navigating workplace conflicts, you can foster a culture of open communication, collaboration, and respect, leading to more harmonious and productive work relationships.

Building a Positive Work Culture

A positive work culture refers to the shared values, beliefs, attitudes, and behaviors that characterize the work environment within an organization. It encompasses the overall atmosphere, norms, and practices that shape the employee experience and influence their attitudes, behaviors, and performance. In a positive work culture, employees feel valued, respected, and supported, and are motivated to contribute their best work towards the organization's goals. Key elements of a positive work culture include open communication, trust, collaboration, recognition, work-life balance, diversity and inclusion, and a focus on employee well-being and development. A positive work culture fosters high levels of employee engagement, satisfaction, and productivity, as well as organizational success and resilience in the face of challenges.

Building a positive work culture is crucial for fostering employee engagement, productivity, and satisfaction, as well as attracting and retaining top talent. Here are some strategies for creating a positive work culture:

1. **Define Core Values:** Establish clear core values that reflect the organization's mission, vision, and principles. Communicate these values to employees and integrate them into all aspects of the organization's culture, from hiring and onboarding to performance evaluations and decision-making processes.
2. **Lead by Example:** Leaders play a critical role in shaping the organizational culture. Lead by example by embodying the values and behaviors you want to see in your employees. Demonstrate authenticity, integrity, and respect in your interactions, and prioritize employee well-being and development.
3. **Foster Open Communication:** Encourage open, transparent communication at all levels of the organization. Create opportunities for employees to share their ideas, concerns, and feedback freely, and actively listen to their input. Establish channels for two-way communication, such as

regular team meetings, suggestion boxes, or anonymous surveys.

4. **Promote Collaboration:** Create a collaborative work environment where teamwork and cooperation are valued and encouraged. Foster cross-functional collaboration by breaking down silos and promoting knowledge sharing and information exchange among teams. Encourage collaboration through team-building activities, workshops, or collaborative projects.

5. **Recognize and Reward Achievements:** Acknowledge and celebrate the achievements and contributions of employees regularly. Recognize their efforts publicly, whether through employee of the month awards, shout-outs in team meetings, or appreciation events. Reward employees for their hard work and dedication through incentives, bonuses, or other forms of recognition.

6. **Support Work-Life Balance:** Prioritize work-life balance and employee well-being by offering flexible work arrangements, such as remote work options, flexible hours, or compressed workweeks. Encourage employees to take regular breaks, vacations, and time off to recharge and avoid burnout. Provide resources and support for managing stress, promoting mental health, and maintaining work-life balance.

7. **Invest in Employee Development:** Invest in employee development and growth opportunities to help employees reach their full potential. Offer training, workshops, or professional development programs to enhance their skills and knowledge. Provide opportunities for mentorship, coaching, or job rotations to facilitate career advancement and skill-building.

8. **Promote Diversity and Inclusion:** Foster a culture of diversity and inclusion where all employees feel valued, respected, and included. Promote diversity in hiring and promotion practices, and create a welcoming and inclusive environment where employees from diverse backgrounds can thrive. Address bias and discrimination proactively and create opportunities for cross-cultural understanding and collaboration.
9. **Encourage Innovation and Creativity:** Create an environment that encourages innovation, creativity, and risk-taking. Empower employees to generate new ideas, experiment with different approaches, and take calculated risks to drive innovation and continuous improvement. Provide resources, support, and recognition for innovative initiatives and successes.
10. **Solicit Feedback and Adapt:** Regularly solicit feedback from employees about the organizational culture, policies, and practices. Use this feedback to identify areas for improvement and adapt the culture to better meet the needs and preferences of employees. Demonstrate a willingness to listen, learn, and evolve based on employee input.

By implementing these strategies, organizations can create a positive work culture that promotes employee engagement, satisfaction, and well-being, as well as organizational success and competitiveness in today's dynamic business environment.

Managing Stress and Burnout

Managing stress and burnout involves implementing strategies to cope with and alleviate the negative effects of stress and prevent the onset of burnout. Stress refers to the body's natural response to challenges or demands, while burnout is a state of emotional, physical, and mental exhaustion often caused by prolonged exposure to stressors.

Managing stress and burnout typically involves a combination of techniques aimed at reducing stress levels, promoting relaxation, and enhancing resilience. This may include strategies such as prioritizing self-care, setting boundaries, practicing time management, seeking social support, engaging in relaxation techniques, and addressing underlying sources of stress.

The goal of managing stress and burnout is to maintain a healthy balance between work and personal life, cultivate resilience in the face of challenges, and prevent the negative consequences associated with chronic stress and burnout, such as decreased productivity, impaired physical and mental health, and diminished job satisfaction. By proactively managing stress and burnout, individuals can enhance their overall well-being and effectiveness in both their professional and personal lives.

Managing stress and burnout is essential for maintaining well-being and productivity in the workplace. Here are some strategies to help individuals effectively manage stress and prevent burnout:

1. **Recognize Early Signs:** Be aware of the early signs of stress and burnout, such as feeling overwhelmed, irritable, or fatigued, and take proactive steps to address them before they escalate.

2. **Set Boundaries:** Establish clear boundaries between work and personal life to prevent work-related stress from spilling over into other areas of life. Set realistic expectations for workload and availability, and communicate boundaries with colleagues and supervisors.

3. **Prioritize Self-Care:** Make self-care a priority by engaging in activities that promote physical, mental, and emotional well-being. This includes getting enough sleep, eating a balanced diet, exercising regularly, and practicing relaxation techniques such as deep breathing or mindfulness.

4. **Manage Workload:** Break tasks into manageable chunks and prioritize them based on importance and urgency. Delegate tasks when possible and communicate with supervisors or colleagues if workload becomes overwhelming.

5. **Practice Time Management:** Use time management techniques such as to-do lists, prioritization, and time blocking to manage tasks effectively and avoid procrastination. Set realistic deadlines and avoid overcommitting to tasks or projects.

6. **Seek Support:** Reach out to colleagues, supervisors, or support networks for assistance and guidance when needed. Don't hesitate to ask for help or delegate tasks if feeling overwhelmed.

7. **Develop Coping Strategies:** Identify healthy coping strategies to manage stress and build resilience. This may include exercise, relaxation techniques, hobbies, or spending time with loved ones.

8. **Limit Exposure to Stressors:** Minimize exposure to stressful situations or environments whenever possible. This may involve setting boundaries with difficult colleagues or clients, avoiding stressful tasks during times of peak stress, or taking breaks when needed.

9. **Practice Mindfulness:** Incorporate mindfulness practices into daily routines to promote self-

awareness, reduce stress, and improve focus and concentration. This may include mindfulness meditation, yoga, or simply taking a few minutes to pause and breathe deeply.

10. **Take Breaks:** Schedule regular breaks throughout the workday to rest and recharge. Step away from your desk, go for a short walk, or engage in activities that help clear your mind and reduce stress.
11. **Seek Professional Help:** If stress and burnout become overwhelming or persistent, consider seeking support from a mental health professional. Therapy or counseling can provide valuable tools and strategies for managing stress and improving well-being.

By implementing these strategies, individuals can effectively manage stress and prevent burnout, leading to greater well-being, productivity, and job satisfaction in the workplace.

8

Emotional Intelligence and Mental Health

Mental health refers to a person's overall psychological and emotional well-being. It encompasses the state of one's mind, emotions, thoughts, and behaviors, as well as their ability to cope with stress, manage emotions, and navigate the challenges of life effectively. Mental health is not just the absence of mental illness but also the presence of positive factors such as resilience, self-esteem, and a sense of purpose and meaning in life.

Good mental health enables individuals to function optimally in their daily lives, maintain fulfilling relationships, and cope with the ups and downs of life with resilience and adaptability. It involves having a positive outlook, a strong support system, and effective coping strategies for dealing with stress and adversity. Mental health is influenced by a combination of genetic, biological, environmental, and psychological factors, as well as life experiences and social determinants such as access to healthcare, education, and socioeconomic status.

Mental health encompasses a wide range of dimensions, including emotional well-being, psychological resilience, cognitive functioning, and social functioning. It involves the ability to manage emotions effectively, cope with stress, maintain healthy relationships, and make sound decisions. Mental health is essential for overall well-being and quality of life, as it impacts every aspect of a person's life, from their physical health and relationships to their work and social interactions.

Promoting mental health involves fostering resilience, building coping skills, reducing stigma and discrimination, and providing access to mental healthcare and support services. It is essential to address the social determinants of mental health, such as poverty, inequality, and social isolation, and to create supportive environments that promote mental well-being for all individuals. By prioritizing mental health and well-being, individuals and communities can thrive and lead fulfilling lives.

The Connection Between Emotional Intelligence and Mental Health

The connection between emotional intelligence (EI) and mental health is profound and reciprocal, with each influencing and impacting the other in significant ways. Here's how emotional intelligence and mental health are interconnected:

1. **Emotion Regulation:** Emotional intelligence involves the ability to recognize, understand, and manage one's own emotions effectively. Individuals with high Emotional intelligence involves are better equipped to regulate their

emotions in response to stress, adversity, and challenging situations. Effective emotion regulation is a key component of mental health, as it helps prevent or mitigate symptoms of anxiety, depression, and other mental health disorders.

2. **Stress Management:** EI skills such as self-awareness, self-regulation, and coping strategies play a significant role in managing stress and promoting resilience. Individuals with high Emotional intelligence are better able to identify stressors, cope with pressure, and maintain a sense of balance and perspective in the face of adversity. This can help reduce the risk of stress-related mental health problems and promote overall well-being.
3. **Empathy and Social Support:** Empathy, another key component of Emotional intelligence involves, involves understanding and empathizing with the emotions of others. Individuals with high Emotional intelligence involves are more likely to form strong, supportive social connections and seek help when needed, which can buffer against feelings of isolation and loneliness commonly associated with mental health problems. Social support is a crucial protective factor for mental health, and Emotional intelligence involves skills can enhance one's ability to seek and provide support effectively.
4. **Interpersonal Relationships:** Emotional intelligence involves plays a critical role in interpersonal relationships, influencing how individuals communicate, resolve conflicts, and build meaningful connections with others. Strong, positive relationships are essential for mental health and well-being, providing emotional

support, validation, and a sense of belonging. Individuals with high Emotional intelligence involves are better equipped to navigate interpersonal dynamics, maintain healthy boundaries, and cultivate fulfilling relationships, which can contribute to overall mental health and resilience.

5. **Self-Esteem and Self-Compassion:** Emotional intelligence involves is closely linked to self-esteem and self-compassion, which are important factors in mental health and well-being. Individuals with high Emotional intelligence involves are more likely to have a positive self-image, practice self-care, and show themselves kindness and understanding during difficult times. Cultivating self-compassion can help protect against feelings of shame, self-criticism, and low self-worth, which are risk factors for mental health problems such as depression and anxiety.

6. **Coping and Adaptation:** Emotional intelligence involves skills such as adaptability, flexibility, and problem-solving can help individuals cope with life's challenges and setbacks more effectively. Resilience, the ability to bounce back from adversity, is a key aspect of mental health and well-being, and Emotional intelligence involves plays a crucial role in promoting resilience by enhancing one's ability to cope with stress, problem-solve, and find meaning and purpose in difficult situations.

Overall, the connection between emotional intelligence and mental health is multifaceted and bidirectional, with each influencing and supporting the other in promoting well-being and resilience. By cultivating emotional intelligence skills, individuals can enhance their mental health and well-being, build stronger relationships, and navigate life's challenges with greater ease and resilience. Similarly, prioritizing mental health can contribute to the development and enhancement of emotional intelligence, creating a positive feedback loop that promotes overall well-being.

Understanding Emotional Disorders

Understanding emotional disorders is crucial for identifying, diagnosing, and effectively treating mental health conditions that affect individuals' emotional well-being. Emotional disorders, also known as mood disorders or affective disorders, are a broad category of mental health conditions characterized by disturbances in mood, emotions, and affect. Here are some key aspects to consider:

1. **Types of Emotional Disorders:** Emotional disorders encompass a wide range of conditions, including:

   - Depression: Characterized by persistent feelings of sadness, hopelessness, and loss of interest or pleasure in activities.
   - Anxiety Disorders: Including generalized anxiety disorder, panic disorder, social anxiety disorder, and specific phobias, these conditions involve excessive worry, fear, or nervousness that significantly impacts daily functioning.
   - Bipolar Disorder: Marked by extreme mood swings between periods of depression and episodes of mania or hypomania, which involve elevated mood, increased energy, and impulsivity.
   - Post-Traumatic Stress Disorder (PTSD): Occurs in individuals who have experienced or witnessed a traumatic event and involves intrusive memories, flashbacks, nightmares, and heightened arousal.

- Obsessive-Compulsive Disorder (OCD): Characterized by recurrent, intrusive thoughts (obsessions) and repetitive behaviors or mental rituals (compulsions) performed to alleviate anxiety.
- Borderline Personality Disorder (BPD): Involves instability in mood, self-image, and interpersonal relationships, as well as impulsive behavior and intense fear of abandonment.

2. **Causes and Risk Factors:** Emotional disorders are influenced by a combination of genetic, biological, psychological, and environmental factors. Genetics, brain chemistry, trauma, stress, early childhood experiences, and personality traits can all contribute to the development of emotional disorders. Additionally, factors such as substance abuse, chronic illness, and social isolation can increase the risk of developing these conditions.
3. **Symptoms:** Symptoms of emotional disorders vary depending on the specific condition but may include:
    - Persistent sadness or irritability
    - Feelings of anxiety, panic, or fear
    - Changes in appetite or weight
    - Sleep disturbances
    - Fatigue or loss of energy
    - Difficulty concentrating or making decisions
    - Suicidal thoughts or behaviors
    - Mood swings or emotional outbursts
    - Impulsive or risky behavior
    - Intrusive thoughts or compulsive behaviors
4. **Diagnosis and Treatment:** Diagnosis of emotional disorders typically involves a comprehensive

assessment by a mental health professional, including a review of symptoms, medical history, and psychological evaluations. Treatment may include a combination of psychotherapy (such as cognitive-behavioral therapy, dialectical behavior therapy, or interpersonal therapy), medication (such as antidepressants, mood stabilizers, or antipsychotics), and lifestyle modifications (such as stress management techniques, exercise, and social support).

5. **Impact on Daily Functioning:** Emotional disorders can significantly impact individuals' daily functioning, relationships, work or school performance, and overall quality of life. They may also increase the risk of other health problems, including substance abuse, chronic medical conditions, and suicide.

6. **Prevention and Management:** Early intervention, effective treatment, and ongoing support are essential for managing emotional disorders and reducing the risk of complications. Prevention efforts may include promoting mental health awareness, reducing stigma, and addressing underlying risk factors such as trauma, stress, and social isolation.

Overall, understanding emotional disorders is critical for promoting mental health, improving diagnosis and treatment, and enhancing overall well-being for individuals affected by these conditions. By raising awareness, reducing stigma, and providing access to effective care and support, we can better address the challenges associated with emotional disorders and help individuals lead healthier, more fulfilling lives.

Practices for Enhancing Emotional Intelligence and Mental Health

Enhancing emotional intelligence (EI) and mental

health involves adopting practices and strategies that promote self-awareness, emotional regulation, social skills, and resilience. Here are some practices for enhancing EI and mental health:

1. **Mindfulness Meditation:** Mindfulness meditation involves paying attention to the present moment without judgment. Regular mindfulness practice can increase self-awareness, improve emotional regulation, and reduce stress and anxiety. It helps individuals become more attuned to their thoughts, feelings, and bodily sensations, promoting overall mental well-being.
2. **Emotion Regulation Techniques:** Learning and practicing emotion regulation techniques such as deep breathing, progressive muscle relaxation, and guided imagery can help individuals manage intense emotions and reduce physiological arousal. These techniques promote relaxation, reduce stress levels, and enhance emotional resilience.
3. **Journaling:** Keeping a journal allows individuals to reflect on their thoughts, feelings, and experiences, promoting self-awareness and emotional processing. Writing about emotions can help individuals gain insight into their emotional patterns, triggers, and coping strategies, leading to greater emotional intelligence and mental clarity.
4. **Social Support:** Cultivating strong social connections and seeking support from friends, family, or support groups can promote emotional well-being and resilience. Spending time with supportive individuals, sharing experiences, and receiving validation and empathy can buffer against stress and promote positive mental health outcomes.

5. **Therapy or Counseling:** Seeking therapy or counseling from a mental health professional can provide individuals with tools and techniques for enhancing emotional intelligence and improving mental health. Therapists can help individuals explore their emotions, develop coping strategies, and build resilience in the face of challenges.

6. **Self-Compassion Practices:** Practicing self-compassion involves treating oneself with kindness, understanding, and acceptance, especially during difficult times. Engaging in self-compassion practices such as self-soothing techniques, positive self-talk, and self-care activities can promote emotional well-being and enhance resilience.

7. **Physical Activity:** Regular exercise has been shown to have numerous benefits for mental health, including reducing symptoms of depression, anxiety, and stress. Physical activity releases endorphins, neurotransmitters that promote feelings of well-being, and can also serve as a healthy outlet for managing emotions and stress.

8. **Healthy Lifestyle Habits:** Adopting healthy lifestyle habits such as getting enough sleep, eating a balanced diet, limiting alcohol and caffeine intake, and avoiding recreational drugs can support overall mental health and well-being. These habits provide a solid foundation for emotional regulation, cognitive functioning, and resilience.

9. **Continued Learning and Growth:** Engaging in activities that promote personal growth and development, such as reading, attending workshops or seminars, or pursuing hobbies and interests, can enhance emotional intelligence and

mental well-being. Learning new skills, gaining new perspectives, and challenging oneself fosters resilience and adaptability.

10. **Setting Boundaries:** Establishing clear boundaries in relationships and commitments is essential for maintaining emotional balance and well-being. Setting limits on time, energy, and resources can help individuals preserve their emotional health and prevent burnout or overwhelm.

By incorporating these practices into daily life, individuals can enhance their emotional intelligence, improve mental health, and build resilience to cope with life's challenges effectively. It's essential to find practices that resonate with personal preferences and needs and to cultivate a holistic approach to emotional well-being and growth.

Mindfulness-Based Stress Reduction (MBSR)

Mindfulness-Based Stress Reduction (MBSR) is a structured program that aims to reduce stress and enhance well-being through mindfulness meditation and mindfulness-based practices. Developed by Dr. Jon Kabat-Zinn in the late 1970s, MBSR integrates mindfulness meditation with elements of cognitive-behavioral therapy, yoga, and body awareness techniques. The program has been widely researched and shown to be effective in reducing stress, anxiety, depression, and improving overall quality of life.

Key components of Mindfulness-Based Stress Reduction include:

1. **Mindfulness Meditation:** MBSR teaches participants to cultivate mindfulness through various meditation practices, including body scan meditation, mindful breathing, and mindful movement (yoga). These practices help individuals

develop present-moment awareness, non-judgmental observation of thoughts and emotions, and acceptance of their experiences.

2. **Body Awareness:** MBSR emphasizes the importance of developing awareness of bodily sensations and using the body as a gateway to mindfulness. Body scan meditation, in particular, involves systematically bringing attention to different parts of the body, noticing sensations, and cultivating a non-reactive awareness of bodily experiences.

3. **Yoga and Gentle Movement:** MBSR incorporates gentle yoga practices to promote relaxation, flexibility, and embodied mindfulness. Yoga poses are practiced mindfully, focusing on the sensations of stretching and movement, and integrating breath awareness with movement.

4. **Mindful Inquiry:** MBSR includes opportunities for reflection and inquiry into one's experiences during mindfulness practices. Participants are encouraged to explore their thoughts, emotions, and physical sensations with curiosity and openness, without judgment or analysis.

5. **Daily Practice:** Participants are encouraged to engage in daily mindfulness practices outside of class sessions, integrating mindfulness into their daily routines and activities. Consistent practice is essential for cultivating mindfulness skills and reaping the benefits of the program.

The MBSR program typically consists of eight weekly sessions, each lasting around 2-3 hours, along with a full-day retreat. Participants learn and practice mindfulness techniques, engage in group discussions and exercises, and receive guidance and support from a trained MBSR instructor. The program emphasizes self-awareness, self-compassion, and non-reactivity to stressors, teaching participants to respond to life's challenges with greater resilience and equanimity.

Research has shown that participation in MBSR can lead to significant reductions in perceived stress, anxiety, and depressive symptoms, as well as improvements in overall well-being, quality of life, and emotional regulation. MBSR has been widely adopted in clinical settings, workplace wellness programs, educational institutions, and community settings as an evidence-based intervention for stress reduction and mental health promotion.

Overall, Mindfulness-Based Stress Reduction offers a holistic approach to stress management and well-being, empowering individuals to cultivate mindfulness skills and develop healthier ways of relating to their inner experiences and external stressors. Through regular practice and ongoing self-exploration, participants can cultivate greater resilience, inner peace, and balance in their lives.

Cognitive-Behavioral Techniques

Cognitive-Behavioral Techniques (CBT) refer to a set of therapeutic interventions and strategies aimed at identifying and modifying patterns of thinking (cognitive processes) and behaviors that contribute to emotional distress and mental health issues. Developed by Dr. Aaron Beck and Dr. Albert Ellis in the 1960s, CBT is rooted in the cognitive theory of psychopathology, which suggests that our thoughts, feelings, and behaviors are interconnected and influence each other.

The core principles of CBT include:

1. **Cognitive Restructuring:** This technique involves identifying and challenging negative or irrational thoughts, beliefs, and assumptions that contribute to emotional distress. By examining

evidence for and against these thoughts, individuals learn to replace them with more balanced and realistic interpretations, leading to changes in emotions and behaviors.

2. **Behavioral Activation:** Behavioral activation aims to increase engagement in rewarding and meaningful activities as a way to alleviate symptoms of depression and improve mood. By scheduling and participating in enjoyable or fulfilling activities, individuals increase positive reinforcement and reduce avoidance behaviors.

3. **Exposure Therapy:** Exposure therapy is used to treat anxiety disorders, phobias, and trauma-related conditions. It involves gradual exposure to feared stimuli or situations, allowing individuals to confront and overcome their fears through repeated exposure and habituation.

4. **Behavioral Experiments:** Behavioral experiments involve testing beliefs or assumptions through real-life experiments or behavioral tests. By gathering evidence and challenging unhelpful beliefs through direct experience, individuals can gain new insights and perspectives, leading to changes in behavior and emotional responses.

5. **Problem-Solving Skills:** Problem-solving skills training teaches individuals practical strategies for identifying, evaluating, and resolving problems in their lives. By breaking down problems into manageable steps and generating alternative solutions, individuals develop more adaptive coping skills and enhance their ability to manage stress and challenges effectively.

6. **Relaxation Techniques:** Relaxation techniques such as progressive muscle relaxation, deep breathing, and guided imagery are used to promote relaxation and reduce physiological

arousal associated with stress and anxiety. These techniques can help individuals manage symptoms of anxiety, improve sleep quality, and enhance overall well-being.

7. **Social Skills Training:** Social skills training focuses on improving interpersonal communication, assertiveness, and relationship-building skills. Through role-playing, modeling, and feedback, individuals learn effective ways to express themselves, set boundaries, and navigate social interactions, leading to improved relationships and social support.

Overall, cognitive-behavioral techniques are evidence-based and widely used in the treatment of various mental health conditions, including depression, anxiety disorders, post-traumatic stress disorder (PTSD), obsessive-compulsive disorder (OCD), and eating disorders. By teaching individuals practical skills for identifying and changing maladaptive patterns of thinking and behavior, CBT empowers them to take an active role in managing their mental health and improving their overall quality of life. Cognitive-behavioral techniques (CBT) are a widely used therapeutic approach that focuses on identifying and changing patterns of thinking (cognitive processes) and behaviors that contribute to emotional distress and mental health problems.

Key cognitive-behavioral techniques include:

1. **Cognitive Restructuring:** Cognitive restructuring involves identifying and challenging negative or irrational thoughts (cognitive distortions) that contribute to emotional distress. Through techniques such as cognitive reframing and thought records, individuals learn to replace unhelpful thoughts with more balanced and realistic alternatives, leading to a shift in emotions and behaviors.

2. **Behavioral Activation:** Behavioral activation aims to increase engagement in rewarding and meaningful activities as a way to alleviate symptoms of depression and improve mood. Individuals identify enjoyable or fulfilling activities and gradually incorporate them into their daily routines, focusing on increasing positive reinforcement and reducing avoidance behaviors.

3. **Exposure Therapy:** Exposure therapy is a behavioral technique used to treat anxiety disorders, phobias, and trauma-related conditions. It involves gradually exposing individuals to feared situations, objects, or memories in a controlled and systematic manner, helping them confront and overcome their fears through repeated exposure and habituation.

4. **Behavioral Experiments:** Behavioral experiments involve testing beliefs or assumptions about oneself, others, or the world through real-life experiments or behavioral tests. By gathering evidence and challenging unhelpful beliefs through direct experience, individuals can gain new insights and perspectives, leading to changes in behavior and emotional responses.

5. **Problem-Solving Skills:** Problem-solving skills training teaches individuals practical strategies for identifying, evaluating, and resolving problems in their lives. By breaking down problems into manageable steps, generating alternative solutions, and evaluating their effectiveness, individuals can develop more adaptive coping skills and enhance their ability to manage stress and challenges effectively.

6. **Relaxation Techniques:** Relaxation techniques such as progressive muscle relaxation, deep breathing, and guided imagery are often used in

CBT to promote relaxation and reduce physiological arousal associated with stress and anxiety. These techniques can help individuals manage symptoms of anxiety, improve sleep quality, and enhance overall well-being.

7. **Social Skills Training:** Social skills training focuses on improving interpersonal communication, assertiveness, and relationship-building skills. Through role-playing, modeling, and feedback, individuals learn effective ways to express themselves, set boundaries, and navigate social interactions, leading to improved relationships and social support.
8. **Mindfulness-Based CBT:** Integrating mindfulness-based practices with traditional CBT techniques can enhance self-awareness, acceptance, and emotion regulation skills. Mindfulness-based CBT incorporates mindfulness meditation, body awareness, and acceptance-based approaches to help individuals develop a non-judgmental and compassionate stance toward their thoughts and emotions.

Cognitive-behavioral techniques are evidence-based and have been shown to be effective in treating a wide range of mental health conditions, including depression, anxiety disorders, post-traumatic stress disorder (PTSD), obsessive-compulsive disorder (OCD), and eating disorders, among others. By teaching individuals practical skills for identifying and changing maladaptive patterns of thinking and behavior, CBT empowers them to take an active role in managing their mental health and improving their overall quality of life.

9

Cultural and Social Perspectives on Emotional Intelligence

Cultural and social perspectives play a significant role in shaping the understanding, expression, and perception of emotional intelligence (EI). Different cultural and social contexts influence how emotions are perceived, valued, expressed, and regulated, leading to variations in the conceptualization and assessment of emotional intelligence across cultures. Here is an overview of cultural and social perspectives on emotional intelligence:

1. **Cultural Variability in Emotional Expression:** Cultures vary in their norms, values, and rules regarding emotional expression. Some cultures encourage open displays of emotion, while others emphasize emotional restraint or suppression. For example, collectivist cultures may prioritize harmony and social cohesion, leading individuals to regulate their emotions to maintain group

harmony, whereas individualistic cultures may value self-expression and assertiveness.

2. **Emotional Display Rules:** Cultural norms dictate acceptable ways of expressing emotions in social interactions. Emotional display rules influence how individuals regulate their emotional expressions in different social contexts. For instance, in some cultures, it may be considered appropriate to express anger or frustration openly, while in others, it may be more socially acceptable to conceal negative emotions and maintain a positive demeanor.

3. **Cultural Models of Self and Others:** Cultural models of self-construal, such as independent versus interdependent self-construal, shape individuals' perceptions of themselves and their relationships with others. In collectivist cultures, where interdependence and social harmony are emphasized, individuals may prioritize empathy, social sensitivity, and relational harmony in their interactions, reflecting aspects of emotional intelligence related to social awareness and relationship management.

4. **Cultural Beliefs About Emotions:** Beliefs about the nature, purpose, and significance of emotions vary across cultures. Some cultures may view emotions as inherently positive and valuable for interpersonal communication and social connection, while others may perceive certain emotions as undesirable or disruptive. Cultural beliefs about emotions influence how individuals perceive and respond to their own and others' emotions, shaping emotional intelligence processes such as emotion recognition and empathy.

5. **Cross-Cultural Measurement of Emotional**

Intelligence: The assessment of emotional intelligence can be influenced by cultural biases and assumptions embedded in measurement tools and instruments. Cross-cultural researchers have highlighted the importance of adapting EI measures to account for cultural differences in emotional expression, communication styles, and social norms. Culturally appropriate assessment tools ensure that EI assessments accurately capture individuals' emotional skills and competencies across diverse cultural contexts.

6. **Cultural Learning and Socialization:** Cultural values, practices, and socialization processes play a role in the development and acquisition of emotional intelligence skills. Children learn about emotions through socialization practices within their cultural context, including parental modeling, cultural rituals, and educational practices. Cultural norms and expectations shape how emotional intelligence is fostered and valued within families, schools, and communities.

7. **Cultural Competence and Adaptation:** Cultural competence in emotional intelligence involves the ability to recognize, understand, and navigate cultural differences in emotional expression and communication effectively. Culturally competent individuals demonstrate sensitivity to cultural norms and values, adaptability in cross-cultural interactions, and the ability to communicate and connect with others across cultural boundaries.

Cultural, and social perspectives on emotional intelligence highlight the importance of considering cultural variability, social norms, and contextual factors in understanding and assessing emotional intelligence. Recognizing the influence of culture on emotional processes and interpersonal dynamics enhances our appreciation of the diversity and complexity of emotional intelligence across different cultural contexts. Culturally sensitive approaches to emotional intelligence promote inclusivity, respect, and understanding in multicultural settings, fostering effective communication, collaboration, and relationship building across cultural boundaries.

Cultural Differences in Emotional Expression

Cultural differences in emotional expression refer to variations in how emotions are perceived, experienced, and expressed across different cultural contexts. These differences are influenced by cultural norms, values, socialization practices, and historical and societal factors. Understanding cultural variations in emotional expression is essential for appreciating the diversity of human experience and promoting cross-cultural communication and understanding. Here are some key aspects of cultural differences in emotional expression:

1. **Display Rules:** Cultural norms dictate acceptable ways of expressing emotions in social interactions, known as display rules. Some cultures encourage open and outward displays of emotion, where individuals freely express their feelings through facial expressions, gestures, and vocal cues. In contrast, other cultures may emphasize emotional restraint or suppression, where individuals are expected to conceal or regulate their emotions, particularly negative emotions, to maintain social harmony and avoid disrupting interpersonal relationships.

2. **Individualism vs. Collectivism:** Cultural variations in individualism-collectivism influence emotional expression patterns. Individualistic cultures, such as those in Western societies, prioritize individual autonomy, self-expression, and personal achievement. In these cultures, individuals may be more likely to express emotions

openly and assertively, reflecting values of independence and self-assertion. In collectivist cultures, such as those in East Asian societies, interpersonal harmony, social cohesion, and group conformity are emphasized. Emotional expressions may be more subdued or regulated to preserve group harmony and avoid causing embarrassment or discomfort to others.

3. **High- and Low-Context Cultures:** Cultural differences in communication styles also affect emotional expression. High-context cultures, such as those in many Asian, Middle Eastern, and Latin American societies, rely on indirect communication and nonverbal cues to convey meaning. In these cultures, emotions may be conveyed subtly through facial expressions, body language, and contextual cues, requiring individuals to be attuned to social and relational dynamics. In contrast, low-context cultures, such as those in many Western societies, prioritize explicit verbal communication and direct expression of emotions, with less reliance on nonverbal cues.

4. **Cultural Values and Emotion Norms:** Cultural values shape the norms and expectations surrounding emotional expression. Cultures differ in their attitudes toward emotions, with some cultures placing greater emphasis on emotional expressiveness, authenticity, and emotional honesty, while others may value emotional restraint, self-control, and emotional moderation. These cultural values influence how individuals perceive and regulate their emotions in social contexts and shape their emotional expression styles.

5. **Gender and Cultural Expectations:** Gender

norms and expectations also influence emotional expression patterns within cultures. In many cultures, traditional gender roles prescribe specific emotional behaviors and expressions for men and women. Cultural stereotypes and gender norms may dictate that men suppress vulnerability and display stoicism or aggression, while women are encouraged to be nurturing, empathetic, and emotionally expressive. These gendered expectations can impact how individuals express and perceive emotions in social interactions.

6. **Cultural Change and Globalization:** Cultural differences in emotional expression are not static but may evolve over time due to processes of cultural change, globalization, and acculturation. Exposure to diverse cultural influences, increased mobility, and technological advancements may lead to shifts in cultural norms, values, and communication styles, influencing how emotions are expressed and interpreted in contemporary multicultural societies.

Understanding cultural differences in emotional expression requires sensitivity to the diverse ways in which emotions are experienced and communicated across cultures. Embracing cultural diversity and adopting a culturally responsive approach to emotional expression fosters empathy, respect, and mutual understanding in cross-cultural interactions, promoting effective communication and interpersonal relationships in multicultural contexts.

Understanding Cross-Cultural Emotional Intelligence

Understanding cross-cultural emotional intelligence (EI) involves recognizing and navigating cultural differences in emotional expression, perception, and regulation across diverse cultural contexts. Cross-cultural EI encompasses the ability to understand and manage emotions effectively in interactions with individuals from different cultural backgrounds, as well as the capacity to adapt one's emotional skills and behaviors to fit cultural norms and expectations. Here are some key aspects of cross-cultural emotional intelligence:

1. **Cultural Sensitivity and Awareness:** Cross-cultural EI begins with cultural sensitivity and awareness, which involves recognizing and respecting cultural differences in emotional expression, communication styles, and social norms. Culturally sensitive individuals demonstrate openness to diverse perspectives, curiosity about cultural practices, and respect for cultural diversity, enabling them to navigate cross-cultural interactions with empathy and respect.

2. **Emotion Recognition and Interpretation:** Cross-cultural EI involves the ability to recognize and interpret emotions accurately across cultural boundaries. Individuals must be attuned to cultural variations in emotional expressions, facial expressions, body language, and vocal cues, as well as cultural context and situational factors that influence emotional experiences. Effective emotion recognition enables individuals to respond appropriately to others' emotional cues and foster empathy and understanding in cross-cultural interactions.

3. **Emotion Regulation and Adaptation:** Cross-cultural EI includes the capacity to regulate and adapt one's emotional responses to fit cultural norms and expectations. Individuals must be able to manage their own emotions effectively in diverse cultural settings, demonstrating flexibility, self-awareness, and emotional resilience. Adaptive

emotion regulation strategies enable individuals to navigate cultural differences in emotional expression, cope with cultural stressors, and build positive relationships across cultural boundaries.

4. **Empathy and Perspective-Taking:** Cross-cultural EI involves empathy and perspective-taking, which enable individuals to understand and empathize with others' emotional experiences from diverse cultural backgrounds. Empathetic individuals demonstrate sensitivity to cultural differences in emotional expression and communication styles, as well as a willingness to perspective-take and see the world from others' viewpoints. Cultivating empathy and perspective-taking promotes mutual understanding, trust, and connection in cross-cultural interactions.

5. **Cultural Competence and Communication:** Cross-cultural EI encompasses cultural competence and effective communication skills, which are essential for building rapport, resolving conflicts, and fostering collaboration across cultural boundaries. Culturally competent individuals demonstrate awareness of cultural norms, values, and communication styles, as well as the ability to adapt their communication approach to fit cultural context and audience preferences. Effective cross-cultural communication promotes clarity, mutual respect, and positive outcomes in intercultural encounters.

6. **Cultural Adaptability and Flexibility:** Cross-cultural EI requires cultural adaptability and flexibility, which involve adjusting one's behavior, communication style, and emotional expression to fit diverse cultural contexts and interpersonal dynamics. Culturally adaptable individuals demonstrate openness to new experiences,

willingness to learn from cultural differences, and ability to navigate unfamiliar cultural settings with confidence and ease. Cultivating cultural adaptability promotes resilience, adaptability, and success in multicultural environments.

Overall, cross-cultural emotional intelligence is essential for navigating the complexities of multicultural societies, fostering inclusive and respectful interactions, and building meaningful relationships across cultural boundaries. By developing awareness, empathy, and cultural competence, individuals can enhance their cross-cultural EI skills and contribute to positive intercultural communication, collaboration, and mutual understanding in an increasingly diverse world.

Impact of Social Norms on Emotional Intelligence

Social norms exert a significant influence on emotional intelligence (EI) by shaping the way individuals perceive, express, and regulate emotions in social interactions. Social norms are unwritten rules or expectations that govern behavior within a group or society, dictating what is considered acceptable or appropriate in various contexts. The impact of social norms on emotional intelligence can be observed in several key areas:

1. **Emotional Expression:** Social norms influence how emotions are expressed and communicated in different cultural and social contexts. In cultures where emotional expressiveness is encouraged and valued, individuals may openly display a wide range of emotions, including joy, sadness, anger, and affection. Conversely, in cultures where emotional restraint or suppression is the norm, individuals may regulate their emotions more closely and exhibit more subdued emotional expressions. Adherence to social norms regarding emotional expression can affect how

individuals perceive and respond to others' emotions, as well as how they express their own emotions in social interactions.

2. **Emotion Regulation:** Social norms also play a role in shaping emotion regulation strategies and coping mechanisms used by individuals to manage their emotions. Cultural norms regarding emotional control, self-discipline, and composure influence how individuals regulate their emotional responses to different situations and stimuli. For example, in cultures that emphasize stoicism and emotional resilience, individuals may be more likely to suppress or minimize outward displays of emotion in response to adversity or stress. In contrast, cultures that encourage emotional expression and validation may promote more adaptive emotion regulation strategies, such as seeking social support or engaging in expressive activities.
3. **Empathy and Social Sensitivity:** Social norms regarding empathy, compassion, and interpersonal sensitivity shape individuals' ability to understand and respond to others' emotions. Cultural expectations regarding empathy vary across cultures, with some cultures placing greater emphasis on empathetic concern and others prioritizing emotional distance or detachment. Adherence to social norms regarding empathy can influence how individuals perceive and interpret others' emotional cues, as well as their willingness to offer support and assistance to those in need.
4. **Socialization and Learning:** Social norms related to emotional intelligence are transmitted through socialization processes within families, schools, and communities. From a young age, individuals

learn about appropriate emotional expressions, communication styles, and relational dynamics through observation, imitation, and reinforcement from caregivers and peers. Cultural values, traditions, and rituals also play a role in shaping emotional norms and expectations within social groups. Over time, individuals internalize these social norms and incorporate them into their own emotional experiences and behaviors.

5. **Cultural Variation:** It's important to recognize that social norms related to emotional intelligence can vary widely across cultures and societies. What may be considered appropriate or desirable in one cultural context may be perceived differently in another. For example, cultural differences in individualism-collectivism, power distance, and masculinity-femininity can influence emotional norms and expectations within social groups. Understanding and navigating these cultural variations is essential for developing cultural competence and effective communication in diverse multicultural settings.

Overall, social norms play a significant role in shaping emotional intelligence by providing guidelines for emotional expression, regulation, and interpersonal communication within social groups and cultural contexts. By understanding and adapting to social norms, individuals can enhance their emotional intelligence skills and build positive relationships with others in a variety of social and cultural settings.

Developing Cultural Sensitivity and Awareness

Developing cultural sensitivity and awareness is essential for fostering respectful, inclusive, and effective interactions in diverse cultural contexts. Cultural sensitivity refers to the ability to recognize, understand, and respect cultural differences, while cultural awareness involves being mindful of one's own cultural biases and assumptions and how they may influence perceptions and behaviors. Here are some strategies for developing cultural sensitivity and awareness:

1. **Educate Yourself:** Take the initiative to learn about different cultures, including their customs, traditions, values, and communication styles. Read books, watch documentaries, attend cultural events, and engage with individuals from diverse cultural backgrounds to gain insight into their experiences and perspectives.
2. **Reflect on Your Own Cultural Identity:** Examine your own cultural identity, including your beliefs, values, and assumptions shaped by your upbringing and experiences. Reflect on how your cultural background influences your perceptions, attitudes, and behaviors toward people from different cultural backgrounds.
3. **Practice Empathy and Open-mindedness:** Cultivate empathy and open-mindedness toward individuals from diverse cultural backgrounds. Put yourself in others' shoes and try to understand their experiences, perspectives, and emotions. Approach cultural differences with curiosity and a willingness to learn rather than judgment or prejudice.
4. **Listen Actively and Respectfully:** Practice active listening when engaging with individuals from different cultural backgrounds. Listen attentively, ask questions, and seek clarification to ensure mutual understanding. Respect others' perspectives, even if they differ from your own, and avoid making assumptions or jumping to conclusions based on stereotypes.
5. **Seek Cultural Experiences:** Seek out

opportunities to immerse yourself in different cultural experiences and environments. Travel to new places, participate in cultural exchange programs, and engage in cross-cultural collaborations to broaden your cultural horizons and deepen your understanding of cultural diversity.

6. **Be Mindful of Nonverbal Communication:** Pay attention to nonverbal cues such as body language, facial expressions, and gestures, which may vary across cultures. Be aware that different cultures may interpret nonverbal cues differently, and strive to adapt your communication style to fit the cultural context.

7. **Ask for Feedback:** Seek feedback from individuals from diverse cultural backgrounds on your cultural sensitivity and awareness. Invite constructive criticism and be open to learning from others' perspectives. Use feedback as an opportunity for self-reflection and growth in your cultural competence.

8. **Challenge Your Assumptions:** Be willing to challenge your own cultural biases, stereotypes, and preconceived notions. Examine how cultural stereotypes and prejudices may influence your perceptions and interactions with others, and strive to overcome them through education, self-awareness, and exposure to diverse perspectives.

9. **Promote Inclusivity and Equity:** Advocate for inclusivity, diversity, and equity in all aspects of your personal and professional life. Take proactive steps to create inclusive spaces where individuals from all cultural backgrounds feel valued, respected, and empowered to contribute their unique perspectives and talents.

10. **Continue Learning and Growing:** Cultivate a lifelong commitment to learning and growing in your cultural sensitivity and awareness. Stay curious, humble, and receptive to new ideas and perspectives, and seek opportunities for ongoing education and cross-cultural engagement.

By actively developing cultural sensitivity and awareness, individuals can enhance their ability to navigate diverse cultural contexts with respect, empathy, and understanding, fostering meaningful connections and collaborations across cultural boundaries.

Techniques for Cross-Cultural Communication

Developing cultural sensitivity and awareness is essential for fostering respectful, inclusive, and effective interactions in diverse cultural contexts. Cultural sensitivity refers to the ability to recognize, understand, and respect cultural differences, while cultural awareness involves being mindful of one's own cultural biases and assumptions and how they may influence perceptions and behaviors. Here are some strategies for developing cultural sensitivity and awareness:

1. **Educate Yourself:** Take the initiative to learn about different cultures, including their customs, traditions, values, and communication styles. Read books, watch documentaries, attend cultural events, and engage with individuals from diverse cultural backgrounds to gain insight into their experiences and perspectives.

2. **Reflect on Your Own Cultural Identity:** Examine your own cultural identity, including your beliefs, values, and assumptions shaped by your upbringing and experiences. Reflect on how your cultural background influences your perceptions, attitudes, and behaviors toward people from different cultural backgrounds.

3. **Practice Empathy and Open-mindedness:** Cultivate empathy and open-mindedness toward individuals from diverse cultural backgrounds. Put yourself in others' shoes and try to understand their experiences, perspectives, and emotions. Approach cultural differences with curiosity and a willingness to learn rather than judgment or prejudice.

4. **Listen Actively and Respectfully:** Practice active listening when engaging with individuals from different cultural backgrounds. Listen attentively, ask questions, and seek clarification to ensure mutual understanding. Respect others' perspectives, even if they differ from your own, and avoid making assumptions or jumping to conclusions based on stereotypes.

5. **Seek Cultural Experiences:** Seek out opportunities to immerse yourself in different cultural experiences and environments. Travel to new places, participate in cultural exchange programs, and engage in cross-cultural collaborations to broaden your cultural horizons and deepen your understanding of cultural diversity.

6. **Be Mindful of Nonverbal Communication:** Pay attention to nonverbal cues such as body language, facial expressions, and gestures, which may vary across cultures. Be aware that different cultures may interpret nonverbal cues differently, and strive to adapt your communication style to fit the cultural context.

7. **Ask for Feedback:** Seek feedback from individuals from diverse cultural backgrounds on your cultural sensitivity and awareness. Invite constructive criticism and be open to learning from others' perspectives. Use feedback as an

opportunity for self-reflection and growth in your cultural competence.

8. **Challenge Your Assumptions:** Be willing to challenge your own cultural biases, stereotypes, and preconceived notions. Examine how cultural stereotypes and prejudices may influence your perceptions and interactions with others, and strive to overcome them through education, self-awareness, and exposure to diverse perspectives.
9. **Promote Inclusivity and Equity:** Advocate for inclusivity, diversity, and equity in all aspects of your personal and professional life. Take proactive steps to create inclusive spaces where individuals from all cultural backgrounds feel valued, respected, and empowered to contribute their unique perspectives and talents.
10. **Continue Learning and Growing:** Cultivate a lifelong commitment to learning and growing in your cultural sensitivity and awareness. Stay curious, humble, and receptive to new ideas and perspectives, and seek opportunities for ongoing education and cross-cultural engagement.

By actively developing cultural sensitivity and awareness, individuals can enhance their ability to navigate diverse cultural contexts with respect, empathy, and understanding, fostering meaningful connections and collaborations across cultural boundaries.

Building Inclusive Emotional Skills

Building inclusive emotional skills involves developing competencies that foster empathy, understanding, and respect for individuals from diverse backgrounds and experiences. Inclusive emotional skills enable individuals to recognize and value the perspectives, emotions, and contributions of others, creating an environment where everyone feels heard, respected, and supported. Here are some strategies for building inclusive emotional skills:

1. **Cultivate Self-Awareness:** Start by cultivating self-awareness of your own emotions, biases, and assumptions. Reflect on your cultural upbringing, personal experiences, and social identities, and how they influence your perceptions and interactions with others. Develop a deeper understanding of your emotions, triggers, and communication style to better manage your responses and behaviors in diverse social contexts.
2. **Practice Empathy and Perspective-Taking:** Cultivate empathy by putting yourself in others' shoes and imagining their thoughts, feelings, and experiences. Practice active listening, seek to understand others' perspectives, and validate their emotions without judgment or criticism. Engage in perspective-taking exercises to broaden your understanding of different cultural backgrounds and social identities, and develop empathy for individuals with diverse lived experiences.
3. **Promote Inclusive Language and Communication:** Use inclusive language and communication strategies that respect diversity and promote belonging. Be mindful of the words and phrases you use, avoiding stereotypes, biases, and microaggressions that may inadvertently marginalize or exclude others. Use language that acknowledges and affirms people's identities, experiences, and emotions, creating a culture of respect, acceptance, and inclusivity.
4. **Value Diversity and Intersectionality:** Recognize and value the diversity of identities, experiences, and perspectives within your community or

organization. Embrace intersectionality by acknowledging the intersecting dimensions of individuals' identities, such as race, ethnicity, gender, sexual orientation, disability, and socioeconomic status. Celebrate diversity as a source of strength and richness, and create opportunities for people with different backgrounds to contribute their unique talents and perspectives.

5. **Foster Inclusive Collaboration and Decision-Making:** Create inclusive spaces where everyone feels empowered to participate, collaborate, and contribute their ideas and perspectives. Foster a culture of psychological safety, where individuals feel comfortable expressing themselves and taking risks without fear of judgment or reprisal. Practice inclusive decision-making by soliciting input from diverse stakeholders, considering multiple viewpoints, and prioritizing equity and fairness in your decision-making processes.

6. **Challenge Bias and Discrimination:** Take proactive steps to challenge bias, discrimination, and exclusion in your personal and professional life. Speak out against injustice, prejudice, and inequity, and advocate for policies and practices that promote diversity, equity, and inclusion. Educate yourself and others about systemic barriers and inequalities, and work collaboratively to dismantle them and create a more inclusive and equitable society.

7. **Build Cross-Cultural Competence:** Develop cross-cultural competence by seeking out opportunities to learn from individuals with different cultural backgrounds and perspectives. Engage in cultural exchange programs, attend diversity training workshops, and participate in cross-cultural dialogues and collaborations.

Cultivate an understanding of cultural norms, values, and communication styles, and adapt your behavior and communication approach to fit diverse cultural contexts.

8. **Promote Emotional Safety and Well-Being:** Create an emotionally safe and supportive environment where individuals feel comfortable expressing their emotions and seeking support when needed. Foster a culture of empathy, compassion, and mutual care, where everyone's emotional well-being is valued and prioritized. Provide resources and support services to promote mental health and resilience, and encourage open dialogue about emotions, stressors, and coping strategies.
9. **Lead by Example:** Lead by example by modeling inclusive behaviors, attitudes, and values in your interactions with others. Demonstrate empathy, respect, and authenticity in your communication and relationships, and actively promote diversity, equity, and inclusion in your personal and professional spheres of influence. Be a vocal advocate for social justice and equality, and use your platform to amplify the voices of marginalized and underrepresented communities.
10. **Commit to Continuous Learning and Growth:** Commit to continuous learning and growth in your journey toward building inclusive emotional skills. Stay curious, humble, and open to feedback, and actively seek out opportunities to expand your understanding of diversity, equity, and inclusion. Engage in self-reflection, seek out diverse perspectives, and challenge yourself to confront biases and assumptions that may hinder your ability to create inclusive spaces and relationships.

By intentionally cultivating inclusive emotional skills, individuals can contribute to creating more welcoming, equitable, and compassionate communities and organizations where everyone feels valued, respected, and empowered to thrive.

10

Measuring and Assessing Emotional Intelligence

Measuring and assessing emotional intelligence (EI) involves evaluating an individual's ability to perceive, understand, manage, and express emotions effectively in various contexts. There are several methods and tools used to measure EI, each with its own strengths, limitations, and applications. Here are some common approaches to measuring and assessing emotional intelligence:

1. **Self-Report Measures:** Self-report measures of EI involve individuals completing questionnaires or surveys designed to assess their emotional abilities, traits, and behaviors. These measures typically ask respondents to rate their own emotional skills, such as self-awareness, self-regulation, empathy, and social skills, using Likert-type scales. Self-report measures are easy to administer and cost-effective but may be

subject to biases, such as social desirability bias, where individuals may provide responses they perceive as socially acceptable rather than accurate.

2. **360-Degree Feedback:** 360-degree feedback assessments involve gathering input from multiple sources, including self-assessment, peer assessment, supervisor assessment, and subordinate assessment, to provide a comprehensive view of an individual's EI competencies. This multisource feedback approach allows for a more holistic assessment of EI skills and behaviors, capturing different perspectives and insights from individuals who interact with the person in various roles and contexts. 360-degree feedback assessments can provide valuable insights for personal and professional development but may be time-consuming to administer and require careful interpretation of feedback data.

3. **Performance-Based Assessments:** Performance-based assessments of EI involve evaluating individuals' emotional abilities through simulated or real-life tasks, role-plays, or situational judgment tests that require them to demonstrate their emotional skills in action. These assessments may involve scenarios such as conflict resolution, team collaboration, customer service interactions, or leadership challenges, where individuals must effectively manage emotions and interpersonal relationships to achieve desired outcomes. Performance-based assessments provide direct evidence of individuals' EI competencies but may be resource-intensive to administer and score.

4. **Ability Tests:** Ability tests of EI assess individuals' capacity to perceive, understand, and manage

emotions through standardized tests that measure specific emotional abilities, such as emotion recognition, emotional reasoning, and emotional regulation. These tests typically involve tasks or items that require individuals to identify emotions in facial expressions, interpret emotional cues in written or verbal scenarios, or demonstrate emotion regulation strategies. Ability tests provide objective measures of EI skills but may have limited ecological validity, as they assess emotional abilities in artificial or contrived settings that may not fully capture real-world emotional challenges.

5. **Behavioral Observations:** Behavioral observations involve assessing individuals' EI skills through direct observation of their emotional behaviors, interactions, and communication patterns in naturalistic settings, such as the workplace, classroom, or social environment. Observers may use structured observation protocols or checklists to document specific emotional behaviors or competencies, such as active listening, empathy, conflict resolution, or leadership effectiveness. Behavioral observations provide rich, qualitative data on individuals' EI skills in real-world contexts but may be subject to observer bias and require trained observers to ensure reliability and validity.

6. **Psychometric Instruments:** Psychometric instruments, such as the Mayer-Salovey-Caruso Emotional Intelligence Test (MSCEIT) and the Emotional Quotient Inventory (EQ-i), are standardized assessments designed to measure various aspects of EI through validated scales or subscales. These instruments typically include multiple-choice questions, scenarios, or statements that assess different facets of EI, such

as emotional perception, emotional understanding, emotional facilitation, and emotional management. Psychometric instruments provide reliable and valid measures of EI but may require specialized training to administer and interpret effectively.

When measuring and assessing emotional intelligence, it is important to consider the purpose of the assessment, the target population, and the specific EI competencies or skills of interest. A comprehensive approach may involve using multiple assessment methods and tools to gather complementary information about individuals' emotional abilities and behaviors, facilitating a more nuanced understanding of their EI strengths and areas for improvement. Additionally, it is essential to interpret assessment results in conjunction with other relevant factors, such as personality traits, cognitive abilities, and contextual factors, to gain a comprehensive understanding of individuals' overall emotional intelligence.

Tools and Techniques for Measuring Emotional Intelligence

Several tools and techniques are available for measuring emotional intelligence (EI), each with its own strengths, limitations, and applications. Here are some common tools and techniques used for assessing EI:

1. **Self-Report Measures:**
   - **Emotional Intelligence Questionnaires:** These questionnaires consist of items that assess various aspects of EI, such as self-awareness, self-regulation, empathy, and social skills. Respondents rate themselves on these items using Likert-type scales. Examples include the Emotional Intelligence Appraisal (EIA) and the Trait Emotional Intelligence Questionnaire (TEIQue).

2. **360-Degree Feedback:**
   - **Multi-Rater Assessments:** 360-degree feedback assessments gather input from multiple sources, including self-assessment, peer assessment, supervisor assessment, and subordinate assessment. This comprehensive feedback provides a holistic view of an individual's EI competencies from different perspectives.
3. **Performance-Based Assessments:**
   - **Simulations and Role-Plays:** Participants engage in simulated tasks or role-plays that require them to demonstrate EI skills in practical scenarios, such as conflict resolution, teamwork, or leadership situations. Observers assess participants' performance based on predefined criteria related to EI competencies.
   - **Situational Judgment Tests (SJTs):** SJTs present participants with hypothetical scenarios and ask them to select the most appropriate response from a set of options. These tests measure participants' ability to apply EI skills in contextually relevant situations.
4. **Ability Tests:**
   - **Mayer-Salovey-Caruso Emotional Intelligence Test (MSCEIT):** The MSCEIT is a performance-based assessment that measures four branches of EI: perceiving emotions, using emotions to facilitate thinking, understanding emotions, and managing emotions. Participants complete tasks that assess their ability to identify emotions in faces, solve emotional problems, and understand emotional dynamics in various situations.

- **Emotional Judgment and Recognition Tasks:** These tasks assess participants' ability to accurately recognize and interpret emotions in facial expressions, vocal cues, or written scenarios. Participants may be asked to identify emotions from photographs of facial expressions or audio recordings of emotional voices.

5. **Behavioral Observations:**

   - **Structured Behavioral Assessments:** Trained observers use structured observation protocols to assess participants' EI-related behaviors in real-life settings, such as the workplace or classroom. Observers rate participants' behaviors on predefined scales that capture aspects of EI, such as empathy, communication skills, and conflict resolution.

6. **Psychometric Instruments:**

   - **Emotional Quotient Inventory (EQ-i):** The EQ-i is a self-report measure that assesses various facets of EI, including self-perception, self-expression, interpersonal relationships, decision-making, and stress management. It provides scores on different EI subscales and a total EI score.

   - **Bar-On Emotional Quotient Inventory (EQ-i):** The EQ-i measures emotional and social functioning across various domains, such as intrapersonal, interpersonal, adaptability, stress management, and general mood. It provides insights into an individual's emotional and social competencies.

7. **Neuroscientific Methods:**

   - **Functional Magnetic Resonance Imaging (fMRI):** Neuroimaging techniques such as fMRI can be used to investigate the neural correlates of EI by examining brain activity associated with emotional processing, regulation, and social cognition. These methods provide insights into the neural mechanisms underlying EI.

When selecting a tool or technique for measuring EI, it is important to consider factors such as the purpose of the assessment, the target population, the desired level of depth and specificity, and the resources available for administration and interpretation. Combining multiple methods and sources of information can provide a more comprehensive understanding of an individual's EI profile and facilitate targeted interventions for EI development. Additionally, it is essential to ensure that assessments are valid, reliable, and culturally appropriate for the intended use and population.

Interpreting Emotional Intelligence Scores and Feedback

Interpreting emotional intelligence (EI) scores and feedback involves understanding the meaning of the scores, identifying strengths and areas for improvement, and using the feedback to guide personal and professional development. Here are some key steps for interpreting EI scores and feedback effectively:

1. **Understanding the Assessment:** Start by familiarizing yourself with the specific EI assessment or tool used to generate the scores and feedback. Understand the constructs, dimensions, and subscales measured by the assessment, as well as the scoring methodology and interpretation guidelines provided by the assessment provider.

2. **Reviewing the Scores:** Examine your EI scores across different dimensions or facets, such as self-

awareness, self-regulation, empathy, social skills, and emotional management. Identify your scores on each dimension and compare them to normative data or benchmark scores, if available, to gauge your relative strengths and weaknesses in different areas of EI.

3. **Identifying Strengths:** Look for patterns or clusters of high scores that indicate your areas of strength in EI. These may include strong self-awareness, effective emotion regulation, empathetic communication, strong interpersonal relationships, or resilience in the face of challenges. Recognizing your strengths can help you leverage them in your personal and professional life.
4. **Identifying Areas for Improvement:** Similarly, identify areas where your scores are lower or indicate potential areas for improvement in EI. These may include deficits in self-awareness, difficulty managing emotions under stress, challenges in understanding others' perspectives, or ineffective communication or conflict resolution skills. Acknowledging areas for improvement is the first step toward developing targeted strategies for growth.
5. **Reflecting on Feedback:** Reflect on the qualitative feedback provided along with your scores, such as narrative comments, observations, or insights from others. Pay attention to recurring themes or specific examples that highlight your EI strengths and weaknesses. Consider how the feedback aligns with your own perceptions and experiences, and be open to new insights or perspectives.
6. **Seeking Clarification:** If you have questions or concerns about your EI scores or feedback, seek clarification from the assessment administrator,

coach, or facilitator. Ask for additional context, examples, or explanations to help you better understand your results and how they were derived. Clarifying any ambiguities or uncertainties can enhance the usefulness of the feedback.

7. **Developing Action Plans:** Use your EI scores and feedback to develop actionable goals and strategies for enhancing your emotional intelligence. Identify specific behaviors, habits, or skills you want to cultivate or improve based on your assessment results. Set SMART (Specific, Measurable, Achievable, Relevant, Time-bound) goals and create a plan for implementing and tracking your progress over time.

8. **Seeking Support and Resources:** Consider seeking support from mentors, coaches, or EI experts who can provide guidance, accountability, and personalized strategies for EI development. Explore resources such as books, articles, workshops, or online courses that focus on building specific EI skills or competencies identified in your assessment feedback.

9. **Practicing and Integrating Skills:** Put your EI development plan into action by practicing and integrating new skills and behaviors into your daily life. Experiment with different techniques for self-awareness, emotion regulation, empathy, and social skills in various contexts, and reflect on your experiences to learn and adjust along the way.

10. **Monitoring Progress and Adjusting Strategies:** Regularly monitor your progress toward your EI goals and evaluate the effectiveness of your development strategies. Adjust your approach as needed based on feedback, observations, and

evolving priorities. Celebrate successes and milestones along the way, and remain committed to lifelong learning and growth in emotional intelligence.

Interpreting EI scores and feedback is an ongoing process that requires self-reflection, openness to feedback, and a commitment to personal and professional development. By leveraging your strengths, addressing areas for improvement, and actively cultivating EI skills, you can enhance your effectiveness, well-being, and success in various aspects of your life.

Using Assessment Results for Improvement

Using assessment results for improvement involves leveraging the insights gained from assessments to identify areas of strength, address weaknesses, and develop targeted strategies for personal and professional growth. Here's how you can effectively use assessment results to drive improvement:

1. **Review Assessment Findings:** Take the time to thoroughly review the assessment results, including scores, feedback, and any accompanying insights or observations. Pay attention to patterns, trends, and areas where you excel or may need improvement.
2. **Identify Strengths:** Acknowledge your areas of strength highlighted by the assessment. These may include competencies, skills, or qualities that contribute to your success and effectiveness in various domains. Recognizing your strengths can help you build on them and leverage them to achieve your goals.
3. **Acknowledge Weaknesses:** Similarly, acknowledge areas where the assessment indicates room for improvement or development. These may include skills, behaviors, or habits that

hinder your performance or well-being. Embrace the opportunity to address these weaknesses constructively.

4. **Set Specific Goals:** Based on the assessment findings, set specific, measurable, achievable, relevant, and time-bound (SMART) goals for improvement. Define clear objectives that align with areas identified for growth and establish concrete steps to work toward them.

5. **Develop Action Plans:** Develop action plans outlining the strategies, resources, and activities you will implement to achieve your goals. Break down your goals into manageable tasks, prioritize them based on importance and urgency, and create a timeline for implementation.

6. **Seek Support and Resources:** Don't hesitate to seek support and resources to help you achieve your improvement goals. This may include seeking guidance from mentors, coaches, or experts in relevant domains, as well as accessing training programs, workshops, or educational materials.

7. **Implement Strategies:** Put your action plans into action by implementing the strategies and activities outlined. Be consistent, disciplined, and committed to following through on your plans, even when faced with challenges or setbacks.

8. **Monitor Progress:** Regularly monitor your progress toward your improvement goals. Track your achievements, milestones, and challenges along the way. Use tools such as progress charts, journaling, or feedback loops to assess your performance and adjust your strategies as needed.

9. **Reflect and Adapt:** Take time to reflect on your experiences, learnings, and outcomes throughout the improvement process. Be open to feedback,

insights, and lessons learned from both successes and failures. Adapt your approaches, refine your strategies, and make necessary adjustments to stay on track toward your goals.

10. **Celebrate Successes:** Celebrate your achievements, no matter how small, as you make progress toward your improvement goals. Recognize and reward yourself for your efforts, perseverance, and accomplishments. Celebrating successes can boost morale, motivation, and confidence as you continue your journey of growth and development.

Using assessment results for improvement is a dynamic and iterative process that requires self-awareness, commitment, and resilience. By leveraging assessment insights to set goals, develop action plans, and monitor progress, you can enhance your effectiveness, well-being, and success in various areas of your life.

Personalized Emotional Intelligence Development Plans

Personalized emotional intelligence (EI) development plans are tailored strategies designed to enhance an individual's EI skills, behaviors, and competencies based on their unique strengths, weaknesses, goals, and preferences. Here's how you can create a personalized EI development plan:

1. **Self-Assessment:** Start by conducting a thorough self-assessment of your current EI strengths and weaknesses. Reflect on your emotional self-awareness, self-regulation, empathy, social skills, and overall emotional well-being. Consider using self-report measures, 360-degree feedback assessments, or performance-based evaluations to gather insights into your EI profile.

2. **Identify Goals:** Based on your self-assessment, identify specific goals for improving your EI. These goals should be relevant, achievable, and aligned with your personal and professional aspirations. Examples of EI goals may include enhancing self-awareness, managing stress more effectively, improving communication skills, or building stronger relationships.

3. **Prioritize Areas for Improvement:** Prioritize the areas of EI that are most critical for your personal and professional development. Focus on addressing the weaknesses or gaps that have the greatest impact on your effectiveness, well-being, and relationships. Consider the context in which you want to apply your EI skills, such as the workplace, relationships, or personal growth.

4. **Set SMART Goals:** Develop SMART (Specific, Measurable, Achievable, Relevant, Time-bound) goals for each area of improvement. Clearly define what you want to achieve, how you will measure progress, and when you aim to accomplish each goal. Break down larger goals into smaller, actionable steps to make them more manageable and achievable.

5. **Identify Development Strategies:** Explore various strategies and techniques for developing EI skills and behaviors. This may include practicing mindfulness and self-reflection, learning emotion regulation techniques, improving active listening and empathy, seeking feedback and coaching, or participating in training programs or workshops focused on EI development.

6. **Create an Action Plan:** Create a detailed action plan outlining the specific activities, resources, and timelines for achieving your EI development

goals. Define the steps you will take to implement each strategy, allocate time and resources accordingly, and establish milestones to track your progress along the way.

7. **Seek Support and Accountability:** Enlist the support of mentors, coaches, or peers who can provide guidance, encouragement, and accountability as you work toward your EI development goals. Share your plan with trusted individuals who can offer feedback, support, and constructive criticism to help you stay motivated and focused.

8. **Practice Consistently:** Commit to practicing and integrating EI skills into your daily life on a consistent basis. Set aside time for regular practice sessions, reflection, and self-assessment to reinforce your learning and track your progress over time. Experiment with different techniques and approaches to find what works best for you.

9. **Monitor and Adjust:** Continuously monitor your progress toward your EI development goals and adjust your strategies as needed. Be flexible and adaptive in response to challenges, setbacks, or changes in priorities. Celebrate your successes and learn from your experiences to refine your approach and keep moving forward.

10. **Evaluate and Reflect:** Periodically evaluate your EI development efforts to assess the effectiveness of your strategies and measure your overall growth. Reflect on your achievements, challenges, and lessons learned, and use this feedback to inform future development plans and goals. Celebrate your progress and acknowledge the positive impact of your EI development journey on your life and relationships.

By creating a personalized EI development plan and committing to consistent practice and reflection, you can cultivate the emotional intelligence skills and competencies needed to thrive personally and professionally. Tailoring your approach to your unique strengths, weaknesses, and aspirations increases the likelihood of success and long-term sustainability in your EI development journey.

Setting Emotional Intelligence Goals Based on EI Assessments

Setting emotional intelligence (EI) goals based on EI assessments involves leveraging insights gained from assessments to identify specific areas for improvement and establish targeted goals for enhancing EI skills and competencies. Here's how you can set EI goals based on EI assessments:

1. **Review Assessment Results:** Start by reviewing the results of your EI assessment, including scores, feedback, and any qualitative insights provided. Take note of areas where you scored high and areas where improvement is needed.

2. **Identify Strengths:** Identify your strengths in EI based on the assessment results. These may include competencies such as self-awareness, self-regulation, empathy, social skills, and resilience. Acknowledge areas where you excel and consider how you can leverage these strengths in your personal and professional life.

3. **Acknowledge Weaknesses:** Acknowledge areas where the assessment indicates room for improvement or development. These may include deficits in self-awareness, difficulty managing emotions, challenges in understanding others' perspectives, or ineffective communication or conflict resolution skills. Embrace the opportunity to address these weaknesses constructively.

4. **Set Specific Goals:** Based on the assessment findings, set specific EI goals for improvement. Define clear objectives that align with areas identified for growth and establish concrete steps to work toward them. Ensure that your goals are specific, measurable, achievable, relevant, and time-bound (SMART).
5. **Prioritize Goals:** Prioritize your EI goals based on their importance and relevance to your personal and professional development. Focus on addressing the most critical areas first, but also consider the interconnectedness of different EI competencies and how improvements in one area may benefit others.
6. **Break Down Goals into Actionable Steps:** Break down each EI goal into actionable steps or milestones. Identify the specific actions, behaviors, or habits you need to develop or change to achieve your goals. Create a timeline for completing each step and establish accountability measures to track your progress.
7. **Develop Action Plans:** Develop detailed action plans outlining the strategies, resources, and activities you will implement to achieve your EI goals. Consider incorporating a mix of self-directed learning, practice exercises, feedback mechanisms, and support systems to support your development efforts.
8. **Seek Support and Resources:** Don't hesitate to seek support and resources to help you achieve your EI goals. This may include seeking guidance from mentors, coaches, or experts in EI development, as well as accessing training programs, workshops, or educational materials focused on building specific EI skills.

9. **Implement Strategies:** Put your action plans into action by implementing the strategies and activities outlined. Be consistent, disciplined, and committed to following through on your plans, even when faced with challenges or setbacks. Practice new skills regularly and seek opportunities to apply them in real-life situations.

10. **Monitor Progress and Adjust:** Regularly monitor your progress toward your EI goals and evaluate the effectiveness of your development strategies. Adjust your approach as needed based on feedback, observations, and evolving priorities. Celebrate your successes and milestones along the way, and remain resilient in the face of setbacks or obstacles.

By setting EI goals based on EI assessments and implementing targeted development strategies, you can enhance your emotional intelligence skills and competencies, leading to improved personal and professional outcomes. Remember to approach your EI development journey with patience, persistence, and a growth mindset, and celebrate the progress you make along the way.

Worksheets and Exercises

EI Development Worksheets and Exercises

Creating EI development worksheets and exercises can be a valuable tool for individuals and groups seeking to enhance their emotional intelligence skills. Here are some examples of worksheets and exercises tailored to different aspects of emotional intelligence:

1. **Self-Awareness Worksheet:**

   Objective: To enhance self-awareness by reflecting on personal emotions, strengths, weaknesses, and values.

   Exercise:

- List five emotions you commonly experience throughout the day.
- Reflect on a recent situation where you felt

particularly stressed or overwhelmed. What emotions were you experiencing? How did you react?

- Identify three of your strengths and three areas for improvement. How do these strengths and weaknesses impact your interactions with others?

2. **Emotion Regulation Exercise:**

   Objective: To develop skills for managing and regulating emotions effectively.

   Exercise:

- Practice deep breathing or mindfulness meditation for five minutes. Notice how it affects your emotional state.
- Identify a specific emotion you struggle to regulate (e.g., anger, anxiety). Write down three strategies you can use to cope with this emotion in a healthy way.
- Create a "stress relief toolbox" containing items or activities that help you relax and unwind. Use this toolbox the next time you feel stressed or overwhelmed.

3. **Empathy Building Activity:**

   Objective: To cultivate empathy and understanding towards others' perspectives and experiences.

   Exercise:

- Practice active listening with a partner. Share a personal experience or story, and have your partner listen attentively without interrupting or offering advice.
- Watch a movie or read a book from the

perspective of a character who is different from you (e.g., different cultural background, life experiences). Reflect on how this experience deepens your empathy and understanding.

- Volunteer or participate in community service activities that expose you to diverse perspectives and experiences.

4. **Social Skills Practice:**

   Objective: To enhance communication, collaboration, and relationship-building skills.

   Exercise:

   - Practice assertive communication by role-playing difficult conversations or scenarios with a partner. Focus on expressing your thoughts, feelings, and needs clearly and respectfully.
   - Join a social or networking group related to your interests or hobbies. Practice initiating conversations, actively listening to others, and building rapport.
   - Reflect on a recent interaction where you encountered a misunderstanding or conflict. What could you have done differently to communicate more effectively and resolve the issue positively?

5. **Stress Management Worksheet:**

   Objective: To develop strategies for coping with stress and promoting overall well-being.

   Exercise:

   - Identify your sources of stress (e.g., work deadlines, relationship conflicts). Rate the intensity of each stressor on a scale from 1 to 10.

- Create a daily or weekly self-care plan that includes activities to promote relaxation, such as exercise, hobbies, spending time with loved ones, or practicing mindfulness.
- Practice reframing negative thoughts or beliefs associated with stressors. Write down a stressful situation and challenge any negative assumptions or interpretations. What more balanced perspective can you adopt?

These worksheets and exercises can be adapted and customized to suit individual needs and preferences. They provide practical tools and activities for developing key emotional intelligence skills and fostering personal growth and well-being. Regular practice and reflection are essential for maximizing the benefits of these exercises and cultivating a higher level of emotional intelligence.

EI Assessment Tools and Questionnaires

Designing effective EI assessment tools and questionnaires requires careful consideration of the key components of emotional intelligence and how they can be measured. Here's a framework for creating EI assessment tools along with examples of questions for each component:

1. **Self-Awareness:**
   - Example Questions:
     1. How often do you recognize and label your own emotions as they arise?
     2. To what extent are you aware of your strengths and weaknesses in personal and professional contexts?
     3. How accurately do you perceive how others perceive you?

2. **Self-Regulation:**
   - Example Questions:
     1. How well do you manage your impulses and reactions when faced with challenging situations?
     2. How often do you practice techniques such as deep breathing or mindfulness to regulate your emotions?
     3. To what extent are you able to adapt to changing circumstances without becoming overwhelmed or stressed?
3. **Empathy:**
   - Example Questions:
     1. How often do you actively listen to others without interrupting or judging?
     2. How well do you understand and consider the perspectives and feelings of others in decision-making?
     3. To what extent do you express empathy and compassion towards others in difficult situations?
4. **Social Skills:**
   - Example Questions:
     1. How effectively do you communicate your thoughts, feelings, and needs to others?
     2. How skilled are you at resolving conflicts and disagreements in interpersonal relationships?
     3. To what extent are you able to build and maintain positive relationships with a diverse range of people?

5. **Emotion Regulation:**
    - Example Questions:
        1. How often do you use strategies such as deep breathing or positive reframing to manage stress?
        2. How well do you control your emotional responses in high-pressure situations?
        3. To what extent are you able to bounce back from setbacks and adversity without becoming overwhelmed?
6. **Overall Emotional Intelligence:**
    - Example Questions:
        1. How would you rate your overall emotional intelligence compared to others?
        2. How satisfied are you with your ability to understand and manage your emotions in daily life?
        3. To what extent do you believe that developing your emotional intelligence could improve your personal and professional relationships?

When designing EI assessment tools and questionnaires, it's important to ensure that the questions are clear, concise, and relevant to the specific components of emotional intelligence being measured. Consider using a combination of Likert-scale questions, open-ended prompts, and scenario-based questions to gather comprehensive data on an individual's EI skills and competencies. Additionally, pilot-testing and validation of the assessment tools can help ensure their reliability and validity in measuring emotional intelligence accurately.

About the Author

Dr. Nupur Gosain has spent nearly a decade helping people understand what truly drives success - not just intelligence, but the ability to understand and manage emotions. Her doctoral research on Mid-Career Transition and Emotional Intelligence sits at the heart of this book.

She is an Assistant Professor of Psychology at the School of Open Learning, University of Delhi, and an Honorary Researcher at the university's Women's Studies and Development Centre. Beyond the classroom, she has taken her message to diverse audiences - from college students on World Mental Health Day to Civil Services Officers at the Ministry of Defence's National Institute of Defence Estates Management, where she spoke on building emotionally intelligent workplaces.

Her work has taken her across borders as well. Through an academic exchange between the University of Delhi and the British Council, she trained at the University of Liverpool, UK, where she also led a workshop helping research scholars manage PhD-related stress and anxiety. She is an alumna of the Intensive Nurturing Future Leadership Programme at IIM Bodh Gaya.

When she isn't teaching or researching, Dr. Gosain is championing a simple idea: that emotional well-being is the foundation of a successful life - at work, at home, and everywhere in between.